THE SELECTED
POETRY OF

GUIDO
CAVALCANTI

THE SELECTED POETRY OF

GUIDO CAVALCANTI

A CRITICAL ENGLISH EDITION

SIMON WEST

t

Published by
Troubador Publishing Ltd
5 Weir Road
Kibworth Beauchamp, Leicester. UK
Tel: (+44) 116 2792299
Email: books@troubador.co.uk
Web: www.troubador.co.uk

Series Editor
Professor George Ferzoco
University of Bristol, UK

ISBN: 9781906510725

Typesetting: Troubador Publishing Ltd, Leicester, UK
Cover photograph by Julia Fuller

CONTENTS

INTRODUCTION

CHAPTER 1. GUIDO CAVALCANTI AND THE *VOCE SBIGOTTITA*

Little is known about the life of Guido Cavalcanti. We have only what can be learnt from a few historical records, anecdotes and character sketches, and from the fifty-two of his poems that have survived since their composition in the second half of the thirteenth century. And yet that little we know is just enough to conjure Cavalcanti as one of the most fascinating figures of his day. We know that he was the dedicatee of the *Vita Nuova*, and close friend of its author Dante Alighieri until their friendship mysteriously ended. We know that he wrote one of the most famous love songs of his day, that he was thought to be haughty in character and a rumoured atheist. We know also that he took part in the political factionalism of his city, and survived an assassination attempt. All the details that have grown up around Guido suggest a larger than life character long before we turn our attention to his poetry.

Cavalcanti's birth date is unclear. He was born in Florence, in all likelihood between 1250 and 1259, to one of the richest and most powerful Florentine families of the thirteenth century. His father, Cavalcante dei Cavalcanti, was an important figure aligned with the White Guelfs. The family was exiled to Lucca in 1260 after the battle of Montaperti, in which the rival Ghibelline faction defeated the Guelfs. But the family came to have a significant role in the running of Florence after the battle of Benevento in 1266, in which the Ghibellines were crushed in turn. Despite the defeat of the Ghibellines, political factionalism continued to dominate the life of the city.

In fact the earliest historical mention of Guido refers to his engagement in 1267 to Bice, the daughter of Farinata degli Uberti, the great Ghibelline leader who had died in 1264. It was a political marriage brokered to keep the peace. Ironically, Dante mirrored this union when he made Guido's father and arch enemy Farinata share a tomb in the tenth canto of the *Inferno*.

It was perhaps inevitable then that Guido, too, would play an active role in his city's political life. Few details have survived. We do know, however, that he participated as one of the Guelf representatives at the signing of peace with the Ghibellines brokered by Cardinal Latino. Four years later he made up part of the Florentine commune's governing body, the *Consiglio Generale*, along with Brunetto Latini and Dino Compagni. Somewhere along the line he did enough to provoke the enmity of Corso Donati, head of the rival Black faction within the Guelfs. The tension between the two men culminated in Corso trying to have Guido Cavalcanti assassinated while the latter was travelling to Santiago de Compostela. The attempt failed, but the highly unstable political situation in Florence led to Guido's exile on 24th June 1300. He was sent to Sarzana, an area known for its malaria. It is probably as a result of malaria that he died on 29th August 1300, just ten days after being recalled to Florence.

One might look to Christopher Marlowe for a similar figure able to combine a most tumultuous political life with poetry of the highest order. As is the case with Marlowe, turning to Cavalcanti's poetry itself for answers is of little help. One is forced to fall back on the character sketch by Boccaccio in *Giornata* VI, *novella* 9 of the *Decameron*. Boccaccio makes Guido the hero of a story on a day whose theme is the *bon mot*. He emphasises Guido's philosophical bent and nobility of spirit:

> *egli fu un de' miglior loici che avesse il mondo e ottimo filosofo naturale … si fu egli leggiadrissimo e costumato e parlante uom molto e ogni cosa che far volle e a gentile uom pertenente seppe meglio che altro uom fare; e con questo era ricchissimo, e a chiedere a lingua sapeva onorare cui nell'animo gli capeva che il valesse.*

> [he was one of the best logicians in the world and a superb natural philosopher … Guido was a most charming and courteous man, and a gifted conversationalist who could do everything he set his mind to and who, better than any other man, knew how to undertake those things which were befitting a gentleman; and besides all this he was extremely wealthy, and thus capable of entertaining as lavishly as you can imagine anyone whom he felt was worthy of such treatment.] (Trans., Musa and Bondanella, The Decameron, Norton, 1982.)

A similar portrait, perhaps the basis for Boccaccio's story, is found in the *Cronica* of Guido's contemporary Dino Compagni where he is described as a 'nobile cavaliere … cortese e ardito ma sdegnoso e solitario e intento allo studio' [a noble horseman … gentlemanly and brave, but haughty and solitary, and focussed on study].

GUIDO AND DANTE

It is not known when Cavalcanti began to write, nor can we date any of his surviving compositions. His immature poems show the influence of the slightly earlier Sicilian School and of Guido Guinizzelli, the precursor of the so-called *Dolce stil novo*, of which more later.

One way to make oneself known as a young poet in thirteenth-century Italy was to write poems addressed to other poets, *rime di corrispondenza*. These epistolary poems usually took the form of the sonnet. They tended to be lighter in tone than the poems addressed to an idealised lady. The epistle might address a specific person, asking for an explanation of some matter concerning the nature of love, or the lover's ideal behaviour. It could be obsequious in tone, or a vehicle for deriding the addressee for a perceived weakness in some amorous or poetic area. To give some idea of the prevalence of the genre, almost one third of Cavalcanti's surviving poems are *rime di corrispondenza*. He shows himself in these poems to be, as both Boccaccio and Compagni presented him, haughty and not afraid to speak his mind. He corresponded by sonnet with many of the major literary figures of the day, including Guittone d'Arezzo, Guido Orlandi, Bernardo da Bologna, Gianni Alfani, Lapo Gianni, and of course with Dante.

It was supposedly as a result of an exchange of sonnets that the friendship between Dante and Cavalcanti began. Dante was born in 1265, making Guido slightly older. Dante tells us at the beginning of the *Vita Nuova* that he met his 'primo amico', or best friend, to whom he dedicated the work, after Cavalcanti responded to his sonnet 'A ciascun' alma presa', which recounts a dream and was sent out for interpretation by fellow poets. Cavalcanti's response was the one that pleased him the most. Whether or not the *Vita Nuova* is an accurate factual account of events is impossible to determine, but it nevertheless remains significant that Dante wanted to present the two poets as closely linked in friendship and in poetic endeavour.

The *Vita Nuova* is an anthology of Dante's lyric poems threaded together by autobiographical commentary. He charts a progression in his attitude to poetry and love that moves steadily, though not without setback, towards the conception we eventually find in the *Commedia*, that is an identification of Beatrice with a divinely sent figure, and poetry as a didactic tool for indicating the path by which to reach her in heaven. Somewhere along this journey Dante seems to have lost his 'primo amico'. Exactly where is difficult to tell. Many scholars have conjectured that a falling out took place between the two friends. There are tantalizing hints in Cavalcanti's sonnets addressed to Dante, but they remain just that.

Another interesting clue is offered by the *Commedia* itself. Cavalcanti does not appear as a character in the *Commedia*, since the temporal fiction of Dante's journey is set around the spring equinox (21st March) of 1300, while Cavalcanti did not die until August of that same year. Yet the two references to him show none of the warmth and friendship one finds in the *Vita Nuova*. The first is Dante's meeting with Guido's father, Cavalcante dei Cavalcanti, in *Inferno* X. The worried parent rises up from a fiery tomb to ask why his son isn't with Dante if the extraordinary journey through the afterlife is made possible by individual genius, *per altezza d'ingegno*. Dante's response is ambivalent, but he says that his journey is dependent on a third party, one whom Guido perhaps held in disdain, 'Da me stesso non vegno: / colui ch'attende là, per qui mi mena / forse cui Guido vostro ebbe a disdegno' (lines 61-63). The second episode is found in *Purgatorio* XI, in the middle of a passage denouncing the search for artistic glorification as an aim in itself, 'così ha tolto l'uno all'altro Guido / la gloria della lingua; e forse è nato / chi l'uno e l'altro caccerà del nido' [So did one Guido, from the other, wrest the glory of our tongue – and he perhaps is born who will chase both out of the nest] (lines 97-99). The two Guidos are, almost certainly, Guinizzelli and Cavalcanti.

Unfortunately it is very difficult to ascertain anything more. Was the falling out based on personal differences, or, as many scholars tend to emphasise, differences concerning poetic practice? Was Cavalcanti's reputed atheism the cause? We cannot say for sure. To our knowledge Cavalcanti produced no edition of his own poetry or any commentary along the lines of the *Vita Nuova* or the *Convivio*. What is quite evident is that the poets held differing views on love. Whereas for Dante love came to be an ennobling and divine force, in Cavalcanti's poetry love is represented as being of this world and rather destructive. Many of his poems chart the irrational and disruptive intrusion of love on the individual. Cavalcanti's is a self-engrossed poetry. There must have been love objects to provoke such suffering, but they never come to life as individuals with biographical details. There is no Beatrice here, for example. Love and the lady or ladies who provoke it are better considered as a representation of irrational forces and the disorder of life. How does the individual deal with such forces? How does language deal with them? Cavalcanti attempts to answer these questions, and he does so in a way that is impossible to reconcile with Dante's mature conception of poetry and life.

When we turn to Dante's early poetry, however, the distinctions with Cavalcanti are not so clear. One thing we can say with some certainty about the two poets is that, in Dante's arrangement of his early poems in the *Vita Nuova*, the similarities in style and language with Cavalcanti's own poetry are most noticeable in the first seventeen chapters. And this might be a good moment to discuss that rather nebulous phrase, the *Dolce stil novo*.

THE DOLCE STIL NOVO

The term *Dolce stil novo*, 'sweet new style', often shortened to *stilnovo*, is traditionally used to refer to a group of Italian vernacular poets who distanced themselves from the earlier tradition centred on the figure of Guittone d'Arezzo (1230-94). They were closer in many ways to the earlier Sicilian School, *scuola siciliana*, a loose grouping of poets who had emerged through the imperial court of Federico II in the first half of the thirteenth century, and who took as their principal model the extraordinarily rich vernacular tradition of lyric poetry which had already arisen through the Provençal troubadours. Where previously Latin was the language adopted for literature of any type, the Sicilian School initiated the Italian vernacular lyric tradition; as their troubadour predecessors had done, they wrote of refined love, *fino amore*, celebrating the beloved lady and describing the effects of love on the narrator.

According to an influential description by the nineteenth-century Italian scholar Francesco De Sanctis in his *Storia della Letteratura Italiana*, the triad of names involved in the *stilnovo* was made up of Guido Guinizzelli (the precursor), Guido Cavalcanti, and Cino da Pistoia. Minor figures included Lapo Gianni, Gianni Alfani and Dino Frescobaldi. Used in this way, as it often is by anthologists to group the above mentioned poets, the term *stilnovo* is misleading because it ignores Dante, who was linked stylistically to the other poets of the *stilnovo* for the early part of his career.

Indeed, it was Dante who coined the term in *Purgatorio* XXIV, line 57, where it is spoken by the character of Bonagiunta da Lucca, who makes no more than a distinction between the new style of Dante and the previous style embodied by Bonagiunta himself, along with Giacomo da Lentini and Guittone d'Arezzo. But even here one must tread carefully since Dante soon distanced himself from

Cavalcanti and turned from the sweet new sound of the *Vita Nuova* poems to the *rime petrose* and the sterner tone of his later canzoni.

Recent scholars have called into question the validity of using the term to denote a literary movement as such. It was a retrospective appellation by Dante . There is no evidence that these writers identified themselves as part of a school. Certainly, there are similarities between them, and in the case of the two major figures, Cavalcanti and Dante, there are strong links between elements of their work. But it is dangerous to think that these writers worked from a common manifesto. The tendency in scholarship today is to treat the term with caution as a vague appellation linking the above named writers, but one which will not do as a substitute for examining the intricate links and differences each poet has with both earlier and contemporary writers inside and outside the category *stilnovo*.[1]

CAVALCANTI AND EARLY ITALIAN VERNACULAR POETRY

It is important to consider the poets of the Italian *Duecento* in relation to their immediate predecessors and contemporaries. A significant proportion of critical work written about Cavalcanti concentrates, in the footsteps of Gianfranco Contini, on tracing echoes of certain acoustic, semantic, or syntactic syntagms through past, contemporary and future poets. Why is this? One reason is the lack of biographical information about individual poets, which can make it hard to know exactly when individual poems were written. Identifying thematic and linguistic similarities with other poets of the period helps us to fill in some of the blanks surrounding Cavalcanti.

Another reason appears to lie in the attitudes of thirteenth-century poets to individual originality. Finding startling new ways of self expression, new themes, new metaphors was not a priority for poets who were already radical in their choice of Italian as a language to write in. They were much more conscious of the need to root themselves in the small but growing vernacular tradition that already existed. On first impression, much poetry of the period can strike a reader today as stylized in language and limited in range to topoi concerning love. Often the love object is an idealized lady noble in both spirit and class, who is out of reach of the narrator. He describes his passion and his efforts to reach her through poetry itself. Of course there were variations on and exceptions to this theme, but nothing which would have prepared contemporary readers for the radical departure undertaken by Dante in the *Commedia*.

In order to have some understanding of how Cavalcanti related to and fitted himself into a tradition of vernacular lyric poetry it is worth examining the work of some of his predecessors. One place to start is with Giacomo da Lentini, the principal voice of the *scuola siciliana*. Giacomo da Lentini, also known as *il Notaio*, or notary, by Dante, was active in the court of Federico II in the years 1233-1240. His poetic output consists of 16 canzoni, 1 discord and 19 sonnets. He is often credited with the invention of this last form. Giacomo, and the other writers who emerged through the imperial court of Federico II, can seem an Italian outpost of Provençal poetry, just as in other parts of Europe around the same time the *Minnesang*, the poetry of the *langue d'oïl*, and the *cantigas de amor*, took their bearings from the same troubadours (Contini 1960 v. 1 45). Many of the central motifs which came to dominate the Italian lyric for some time found one of their first expressions in Italy in Giacomo da Lentini's verse.

Giacomo's most famous canzone, 'Madonna, dir vo voglia', uses topoi that will preoccupy Cavalcanti, particularly in those poems in part 3. One of the most prevalent is the nexus between life, love and death:

oi lasso, lo meo core
che 'n tante pene è miso
che vive quando more
per bene amare, e teneselo a vita.
Donqua mor'u viv'eo?
No; ma lo core meo
more più spesso e forte
che no faria di morte – naturale [lines 5-12].

[Oh, my wretched heart!
which endures such great sufferings
that it lives when it is dying,
because it loves intensely, and yet it regards this as life.
And so, am I dying or am I alive?
Not dying, but my heart
dies often and suffers more cruel pain
than it would through natural death.]
(Trans., Jensen, *The Poetry of the Sicilian School*, Garland, 1986.)

This is echoed in the opening to Cavalcanti's poem 13, 'Quando di morte mi conven trar vita'. But the same canzone by Giacomo also contains the theme of the lady's haughtiness, 'per voi, donna, cui ama [il cuore], / più che se stesso brama, / e voi pur lo sdegnate' [for you, my lady, whom it [my heart] loves / more than itself, it is yearning, / yet you scorn it] [lines 13-15]; the narrator's incapacity to describe love and its effects, 'Lo meo 'namoramento / non po' parire in detto', [My passion / cannot be expressed in words] [lines 17-18]; the destructive nature of love, 'Lo vostr'amor che m'ave / in mare tempestoso' [My love for you which holds me / on a stormy sea] [lines 49-50]; and finally, the narrator's inability to abandon love, despite having recognised its destructive nature, 'perché no mi 'nde lasso? / Non posso: di tal guisa Amor m'ha vinto'. [why don't I give it up? / I cannot: in such a way has Love vanquished me!] [lines 71-72]. All these motifs are central to the poetry of Cavalcanti.

Another succinct early expression of the theme of love's bitterness is found at the conclusion of the long anonymous poem *Mare amoroso*:

> *io farei scrivere nella mia tomba*
> *una scritta che direbbe così:*
> *'Chi vuole amare, li convien tremare,*
> *sì come 'l marinaio in mare amaro;*
> *e chi no'm crede, mi deggia mirare,*
> *ché per amor son morto in amarore* [lines 327-332].

> [I would have written on my tombstone
> a phrase which said:
> 'Whoever would love, must needs tremble,
> just as the sailor in a bitter sea;
> and whoever does not believe me, must need only look at me,
> who for love has died in bitterness.]

Both the bellicose imagery adopted to describe the process whereby love enters the lover, and the use of poetry as a means for soliciting mercy, were aspects of the topos, and are employed by Cavalcanti.

Of course these topoi had very long histories that predated the Sicilian School and their troubadour models. For example, the play on the orthographic and acoustical similarities between the nouns for 'love' and 'bitterness', *amor* and *amarore*, in the *Mare amoroso* is found as early as the Latin playwright Plautus. It is present again in Thomas of Britain's mid-twelfth century version of Tristan, and by the thirteenth century it is a topos that has been fully integrated into the *artes versificandi* (Rossi, 2002, 13). Personal experience may have taught these poets that a similarity existed between love and bitterness, but they enjoyed contemplating the possibility that it may have been reinforced by language itself, summed up in the dictum Dante quotes in chapter 13 of the *Vita Nuova, nomina sunt consequentia rerum.* Today we are less likely to accept as a general rule that the names of things are a reflection of the things themselves, but our continued delight in, for example, rhyme, anagrams, and onomatopoeia is evidence of the desire to create meaningful links both between signifiers, and between the signifier and the thing signified.

CAVALCANTI'S ORIGINALITY

It is all very well to trace such topoi back through a literary tradition, but how exactly were they adopted by Cavalcanti? By turning the topos of *amore-amaro* to his own needs, Cavalcanti wrote some of his most original compositions. He focused on tracing the effects of love in the lover by using the coordinates of the narrator's own psycho-physical responses. This could be said to make up the dominant theme of approximately half the corpus, and in the following selection it is most prominent in those poems in parts 3 and 7. The scholar who has best identified the originality with which Cavalcanti adopts such tropes is Maria Corti. Corti observes that in Cavalcanti, 'si assiste a un continuo processo di ridistribuzione degli elementi di pochissimi campi semantici, a una ristrutturazione del materiale tematico e lessicale prestilnovistico e stilnovistico, notevolmente ridotto' [one is witness to a process of continual redistribution of elements within a very narrow semantic range, and to the restructuring of a remarkably restricted thematic and lexical material from the stilnovo and pre-stilnovo periods] (Corti, 1978, 14). The same elements – the *core*, the *anima* and the *mente* [the heart, soul and mind], for example – reappear in poem after poem, leading to a sense of claustrophobia on a lexical and thematic level which mimics that of the narrator engulfed by love. At the same time Corti identifies a new theatrical tension in the poetry due to a dualism between an ideal metaphysical conception of love and its passionate physical expression in the sensitive soul, the heart and the spirits. According to Corti, this tension rests in 'l'irreparabile contrasto fra la figura ideale della donna, che prende vita nella mente, e l'amore sensibile, cioè l'apporto passionale dell'anima sensitiva, del cuore e degli spiriti vitali all'interiore vicenda amorosa' [the unreconcilable contrast between the ideal figure of the lady, nourished in the mind, and the physical nature of love, that is the passionate contribution made by the sensitive soul, the heart and the vital spirits to this interior amorous adventure]. The result is a continual rewriting or reconfiguring of key elements in a sort of literary kaleidoscope, a 'raffinatissimo gioco combinatorio di unità semantiche, di volta in volta sinonimi o antonimi, che lentamente creano nel lettore l'appropriato orizzonte d'attesa, donde lo straordinario fascino di questa altissima poesia' [a highly refined game of combinations of semantic units, now synonyms, now antonyms, that eventually create in the reader an appropriate horizon of expectation, from which derives the extraordinary interest of this wonderful poetry] (Corti 14).

Such closely drawn thematic and lexical boundaries often find the Cavalcantian narrator in a state of despair, from which his only recourse is to write: writing is a testimony to his predicament, but also a plea for requital to the beloved lady. The plea is nearly always ignored, and sometimes results in what are both passionate and, given the context, extremely dramatic outbursts of frustration, as witnessed in poems 9 and 12, 'Tu m'hai sì piena di dolor la mente' and 'Perché non fuoro a me gli occhi dispenti'. In these cases one is struck by the haughty nature of a narrator ready to embrace death rather than let Love have the last word, 'e se non fosse che 'l morir m'è gioco, / fare' ne di pietà pianger Amore' [and death's truce weren't all that I admire / I'd make Love weep with pity to look on me] from 'Poi che di doglia cor conven ch'i' porti'.[2]

GUINIZZELLI AND GUITTONE
Haughtiness and that disdain which Dante talked of distinguish Cavalcanti from the imposing figure of Guido Guinizzelli. Guinizzelli, born around 1240-45 (some scholars suggest as early as 1230), was active in Bologna until his exile in 1274 and death within the next two years. In *Purgatorio* XXVI, lines 97-99, Dante speaks of him in ecstatic terms as 'il padre / mio e de li altri miei miglior che mai / rime d'amor usar dolci e leggiardre' [the father of me and of the others – those, my betters – who ever used sweet, gracious rhymes of love]; and he was also clearly the paternal voice for many of the *stilnovisti*. In the canzone 'Tegno de folle

'mpres', a lo ver dire' [I think a man foolish, to tell the truth] the themes are again centred on questions of love, but Guinizzelli is representative of a more submissive and sedate spirit than that found in Cavalcanti:

Amor m'à dato a madonna servire:
o vogl'i' o non voglia, così este;
né saccio certo ben ragion vedere
sì como sia caduto a 'ste tempeste:
da lei non ò sembiante
ed ella non mi fa vit' amorosa
perch'eo divegn' amante,
se non per dritta forza di valore,
che la rende gioiosa;
onde mi piace morir per su' amore [lines 41-50].

[Love has granted me to serve my lady,
whether I want to or not, so let it be.
Nor do I see any reason surely
how I've fallen in this grief:
I get no look from her
and she gives me no loving glance
by which I might become her lover,
unless it is the pure force of Love's power
that fills her with joy.
For that I'd gladly die for love of her.]
(Trans., Edwards, *The Poetry of Guido Guinizzelli*, Garland, 1987.)

The motifs that run through Guinizzelli's canzone – the war imagery, the passivity of the lover, for example – are also common to Cavalcanti, yet there is a sense of resignation in the older Guido, a propensity to generalise personal feeling into a single word, *tempesta*. The following lines from Guinizzelli, this time from 'Madonna, il fino amore ch'io vi porto' [My lady, the perfect love I offer you], also talk of unrequited love in humble terms:

Ahi Deo, non so ch'e' faccia ni 'n qual guisa,

> *ché ciascun giorno canto a l'avenente,*
> *e 'ntenderme non pare:*
> *ché 'n lei non trovo alcuna bona entisa*
> *und' ardisc' a mandare umilemente*
> *a lei merzé chiamare* [lines 61-66].

> [Oh God, I don't know what to do or how.
> Each day I sing to this charming lady;
> she doesn't seem to hear me,
> for I find no encouragement from her
> by which I might dare to sue humbly
> and claim mercy from her.]

In this respect Guinizzelli is the bridge between Cavalcanti and the earlier figure of Guittone d'Arezzo. Guittone wrote approximately 300 poems, half of which were courtly love poems, and half moralizing pieces written following his religious conversion to the Milites Beatae Virginis Mariae in 1265. Even his earlier poems, however, are infused with a sobriety and austerity that is absent from Cavalcanti.

SBIGOTTIMENTO AND PERSONIFICATION

Above all, the voice that dominates the poetry of Cavalcanti is one which, despite its eloquence and wit, suffers continual *sbigottimento*. This term is used frequently by Cavalcanti to express the severe shock and bewilderment of the lover and his incapacity to react, having experienced the force of love. The shock stuns the lover, but there is also a sense of alarm and panic inherent in the word. One of the major rhetorical techniques used by Cavalcanti to express this state is that of personification. His poems are characterised by the personification of various internal psycho-physical elements of the individual. The eyes, the heart, the soul, the mind, and the spirits are key characters. They often express opposing states of being, leading to a situation of dramatic tension, as they seem to act out the contradictory nature of the individual. While such motifs were found previously in vernacular poetry, Cavalcanti pushed them to new lengths, and made such personification a driving force for much of his writing.[3] Three hundred years later Shakespeare adopted the same terms to describe internal struggle in sonnet XLVI,

'Mine eye and heart are at a mortal war, / How to divide the conquest of thy sight; / Mine eye my heart thy picture's sight would bar, / My heart mine eye the freedom of that right'.

CAVALCANTI AND THE SPIRITS

It is worth looking closely at one particular element of the personification process: spirit. Like *sbigottimento*, *spirito* is a key word for Cavalcanti, central to his theme of the schizoid individual. We find the word once in the work of his predecessor Guido delle Colonne and once again in that of Guido Guinizzelli; in the fifty-two poems by Cavalcanti, however, *spirito* recurs forty-five times.[4] Throughout Dante's lyric poetry (a body of work twice as long as that by Cavalcanti) we find it twenty-three times, and these are concentrated in the first fourteen chapters of the *Vita Nuova*.[5]

Clearly *spirito* is an important term. Its intended meaning is not that of the theological sense conveyed by the word 'soul', nor does it refer to the third part of the Trinity, though these will be the principal meanings when Dante uses the term in the *Commedia*. The predominant sense is that which Cavalcanti adopted from the natural philosopher Albert the Great:

> *In corpore omnis animalis est corpus subtile quod vocatur spiritus ... Est igitur instrumentum animae directum ad omnes operationes eius ... et est vehiculum vitae et omnium operationum vitae, quae est ab anima, et omnis virtutum eius* [in Contini, 1960, v. 2 497].

> [In the body of all animals there is a subtle body that is called spirit ... It is an instrument of the soul and is in charge of all its operations ... and it is the vehicle of life and every operation necessary for life.]

The spirits were minute and invisible substances working in human beings; in the words of Foster and Boyde, they were 'the carriers of psycho-physical life' (Foster and Boyde 80), what today we might call one's life-force, though to Cavalcanti and his contemporaries the spirits were actual substances and more precisely defined than this English term denotes.[6]

If the spirits are essential to the normal functioning of the body, then it is not surprising that in the poetry of Cavalcanti *sbigottimento* is demonstrated, and enacted to dramatic effect, through a dysfunction of the spirits. Lines such as the following are not uncommon: 'Amore ruppe / tutti miei spiriti a fuggire' [Love forced all my spirits to flee] (poem 10); or 'E dico che miei spiriti son morti' [And I say that all my spirits are dead] (poem 11). In poem 7 the sonnet is addressed directly to the poet's own spirits, which are asked to comfort the narrator himself by sending out from the mind 'parole adornate / di pianto, dolorose e sbigottite' [words adorned with tears, painful and shocked]. Similarly, Dante at the beginning of the *Vita Nuova* gives a long description of the spirits' trembling, crying, and speaking in Latin, as a response to the first appearance of Beatrice.[7]

POET OR NATURAL PHILOSOPHER?

I began this discussion of spirits by quoting the natural philosopher Albert the Great, and in many of the examples from Guido's poetry discussed *spirito* seems to be used with scientific or physiological precision, as if the term has been lifted directly from the context of natural philosophy. It was this that led De Sanctis to describe the *stilnovisti*, and particularly Cavalcanti, as scientists first and poets second. Certainly Cavalcanti did seek to chart his internal passions with something like scientific accuracy; but it is worth noting that there are in fact other rhetorical devices at work which characterise these writings as poetry rather than natural philosophy. Most notable among these is the personification of the spirits. Dante has them speaking in Latin, while in Cavalcanti they run away in fear or are the addressee of a sonnet. This dramatisation of the poet's individual faculties is one example of the poetry at work. Secondly the rhetorical device of overstatement plays an important role. Obviously when Cavalcanti says 'my spirits are dead', 'i miei spiriti son morti', the death is metaphorical and we have therefore moved away from the literal meaning of spirit as it might be used by a natural philosopher. Death is often the point to which the internal *sbigottimento* of the poet leads. At this point in Cavalcanti's work, the precision of description through technical language gives way; it is here that the science stops and the vanishing point which is the realm of poetry begins.

LOVE AT FIRST SIGHT

Some of the most important spirits were the visual spirits, *spiriti visivi*, a division of the sensitive spirits, because of the centrality of sight in the Aristotelian conception of the birth of love. It was through the eyes that Love, itself in the form of a spirit, entered the lover and usurped the lover's own spirits. This is the case in poem 17, which begins 'Pegli occhi fere un spirito sottile', and where the *spirito sottile* is the vision of the *donna*. In using the spirits to describe the apprehension of the lady by the senses, the lover is passive: a material, though invisible, spirit was thought to pass from the loved object to the lover where it would take control.

The visual sense predominated, but the process was sometimes described more generally, as, for example, in Dante's celebrated sonnet 'Tanto gentile e tanto onesta pare': 'E pare che de la sua labbia si mova / un spirito soave pien d'amore / che va dicendo a l'anima: "Sospira"' [and from her lips seems to come a spirit, gentle and full of love, that says to the soul: 'Sigh']. There is something similar in the first line of poem 15 ('Un amoroso sguardo spiritale') and in the opening of poem 16 ('Veggio negli occhi de la donna mia / un lume pien di spiriti d'amore'). Such examples, which talk of external spirits influencing the lover, are generally found in praise poems because it is the pleasure which they inspire that causes the lover's attraction to the loved object. It is what such spirits do once they enter the lover and take control that Cavalcanti exploited and made the trademark of his poetry, as the contrast in tone between the two quatrains in poem 15, a sonnet, indicates:

> *Un amoroso sguardo spiritale*
> *m'ha renovato Amor, tanto piacente*
> *ch'assa' più che non sòl ora m'assale*
> *e stringem'a pensar coralmente*
>
> *della mia donna, verso cu' non vale*
> *merzede né pietà né star soffrente,*
> *ché soventora mi dà pena tale,*
> *che 'n poca parte il mi' cor vita sente.*

The term *spiriti* was sometimes used to describe all the lover's various internal spirits. In this context they tended to be grouped together as vital spirits, and were therefore linked to the heart, which was of central importance in the physiological functioning of the body and of Love's conquest of the lover. We may recall, for example, the definition given by Dante in his poetic manifesto and self-commentary, the *Convivio* [II, xiii, 24]: 'li spiriti umani che quasi sono principalmente vapori del cuore' [the human spirits which are above all vapours in the heart]. In Cavalcanti's poem 14 a similar use of the term is found: 'De la gran doglia che l'anima sente / si parte da lo core uno sospiro / che va dicendo «spiriti, fuggite»' [Out of the great grief that the soul feels, a sigh issues forth from the heart that says continually, 'Spirits, flee']. In poem 22 Cavalcanti writes, 'e senti come 'l cor si sbatte forte / per quel che ciascun spirito ragiona' [and fell the way my heart beats out of control because each vital spirit speaks of strife], where *ragionare*, 'to reason', is a synonym for 'to say', which is itself, in Cavalcanti, often associated with the manifestation of passion. On rare occasions *spirito* stands for the whole individual, a meaning more commonly found in the *Commedia*. This is the case in poem 3 by Cavalcanti, 'riguarda se 'l mi' spirito ha pesanza' [consider how my own spirit suffers].

The term spirit, then, was used with a variety of meanings, many of which take us some distance from the shperes of meaning current today. Traces are still present in expressions such as 'to be in high spirits'; and may be found frequently in Shakespeare, for example, *King Lear* IV, ii, 'This kiss, if it durst speak / would stretch thy spirits up into the air'; and *As You Like It*, III, v, ''Tis not your inky brows, your black silk hair / Your bugle eyeballs, nor your cheek of cream / That can entame my spirits to your worship'.

The personification of an individual's psycho-physical elements in this way gives form to what we might today call feelings or states of mind; at the time, however, they were widely accepted terms of natural philosophy. Personification may appear a technique for distancing the narrator from his own feelings in order to observe these more objectively, and yet, there is often an intense sense of claustrophobia in Cavalcanti's poems that comes from a refusal to look outwards to the external world.

THE CORPUS OF CAVALCANTI'S POETRY

As is true of the work of many thirteenth-century authors, the corpus of Cavalcanti's poetry is by no means authoritative. None of the fifty-two extant poems widely accepted to have been written by Cavalcanti can be dated; nor do they exist in a definitive version. To our knowledge Cavalcanti produced no edition of his own poetry or any commentary along the lines of the *Vita Nuova* or the *Convivio*. Those compositions which have survived do so in numerous manuscripts, the earliest of which can be dated to approximately 1310, a decade after the poet's death. In most cases the manuscripts are anthologies of various poets writing in vernacular during the *Duecento*. They were compiled anonymously, using unknown selection criteria, at the behest of wealthy patrons. Each manuscript page was made from parchment – an expensive material to produce. Some manuscripts printed whole quatrains as one line, and removed spaces between words and even punctuation. Interestingly, the rhyme words at the end of each line had an even greater importance in such an arrangement, the rhyme acting as a signal to the reader of divisions which the eye couldn't pick up on the page.

Cavalcanti's poems are spread over a number of manuscripts. Some poems were misattributed, and where a composition exists in multiple manuscripts there are commonly textual variations.[8] What we can say, however, given the frequency with which works by Cavalcanti appear (especially the canzone 'Donna me prega'), is that it is clear that his writing was already widely regarded from at least the first half of the fourteenth century.

The poems were arranged by type of composition: canzoni first, by all authors, because they were considered the most noble, then ballads, and finally sonnets, which were thought a minor form (though Cavalcanti's own use of the ballad and sonnet testifies to the beginning of a change in attitudes).

The first printed book containing Cavalcanti's poetry was *Sonetti e canzoni di diversi autori toscani in dieci libri raccolte*, published in Florence in 1527 by *li eredi di* Filippo di Giunta. This included twenty-seven compositions by Cavalcanti (one of which was wrongly attributed to Dante, while another was unattributed). It was not until 1813 that the first attempt at an edition dedicated to Cavalcanti appeared, *Rime di Guido Cavalcanti edite e inedite*, edited by Antonio Cicciaporci. The first significant critical edition was *Le rime di Guido Cavalcanti*, edited by Nicola Arnone in 1881.

It is really only in the last fifty years that Cavalcanti has begun to receive the critical attention he deserves. In this period some outstanding Italian editions of Cavalcanti's poetry have been published. The first of these was by Guido Favati. His 1957 edition, *Rime*, examined the textual history of each composition in great detail, and drew attention to a range of manuscript discrepancies. Favati ordered the poems thematically, making chronological arrangements only where stylistic indications permitted doing so. This ordering has been followed by subsequent editors.

In 1960 Gianfranco Contini's anthology *Poeti del Duecento*, presented

Cavalcanti's poems with a few minor changes made to Favati's texts. More recently in 1986 Domenico De Robertis published what has become the standard Italian edition, *Rime. Con le rime di Iacopo Cavalcanti*. This version is based on the Favati-Contini editions, though, once again, it includes some minor textual changes. It is a great work of scholarship, in large part due to the annotations and exegeses accompanying each poem. I have been greatly indebted to the De Robertis edition over the course of my work on Cavalcanti. In 1993 Letterio Cassata published a further edition of Cavalcanti's poetry. This book contains fewer annotations, most of which seek to highlight the influence of earlier writers on Cavalcanti, as well as the influence Cavalcanti himself had on later writers. It does, however, offer alternative readings of the manuscripts in some important passages.

A NOTE ON THE PRESENT SELECTION AND ARRANGEMENT

The Selected Poetry of Guido Cavalcanti includes annotated English and Italian versions of a selection of twenty-three poems by Cavalcanti. This represents just under half his known verse. The aim of the selection has been to include Cavalcanti's best poetry, and at the same time to offer a concise representation of the range of thematic and stylistic elements and genres present in the corpus. The selection includes early poetry, the famous canzone 'Donna me prega', and the best of the poems of *sbigottimento* and praise. In the case of the correspondence sonnets I have focussed on those poems written to Dante. Many of the other correspondence poems by Cavalcanti are obscure because we know little of the addressee or the context in which they were written. The exchange with Dante is by far the longest and richest.

It may be asked why this book is a selection, when the corpus of Cavalcanti's poetry is relatively small. The aim of a selection is to focus attention on the very best poems. This selection covers all the important thematic and chronological stages of Cavalcanti's poetry, at least as far as these latter can be determined. The reader is not burdened by the repetitive nature of some poems, nor by the opaqueness of some of the correspondence sonnets. Instead, the major achievements can be seen clearly. This also allows for a more thorough analysis and discussion of individual poems and their translation than in any previous English edition. Finally, it is worth remembering that a complete edition is impossible. No edition of Cavalcanti's poetry will ever be comprehensive, because no single authoritative manuscript survives, and we have no way of knowing how many of his poems were lost.

A new feature of this particular edition is the way the poems have been grouped. The groupings are thematic, and within each group the ordering follows that of previous editions. Obviously, such an arrangement is artificial, in so far as it cannot reflect Cavalcanti's actual practice. But given the impossibility of establishing how Cavalcanti might have ordered his own work, this approach seems a valid one, and has the advantage of highlighting links between various compositions. The introduction to each of the seven parts justifies the selection in more detail, and where appropriate discusses related poems not included in the present selection.

CHAPTER 2. *TU PUOI SICURAMENTE GIR, CANZONE*: METRE AND FORM IN CAVALCANTI'S POETRY

Sound and rhythm are intrinsic elements in poetry. In Italian poetry of the thirteenth century sound and rhythm were felt to be beautiful when ordered by metre and given structure by form. Ordered language was considered beautiful, not only because it produced sweet sounds, but also because it gave the impression that reality itself could be controlled, or as a medieval poet would have conceived things, poetry reflected the order that was hidden in reality.

It is important for a reader to have some understanding of the metre and form of individual poems by Cavalcanti. Furthermore a structural analysis of individual poems is an important part of the work of the translator. Of course it was precisely these elements of sound, metre and form that Dante singled out when describing the impossibility of translating poetry in *Convivio*, I, vii, 14: 'E però sappia ciascuno che nulla cosa per legame musaico armonizzata si può de la sua loquela in altra transmutare, sanza rompere tutta sua dolcezza e armonia'. [And therefore let it be known that nothing that is made from the musical links of harmony can have its speech transformed without destroying all of its sweetness and harmony.]

While such musical elements may not be translatable, the reader can be made aware of their existence and function in the original, and, where possible, the translator can seek alternative methods of conveying a similar sweetness and harmony. To this end, each annotated poem includes a note on significant structural features. But it is worth introducing the important issues here. For the purpose of highlighting certain metrical elements, the progression of sound and rhythm in a given line will need to be separated in the following discussion from the meaning of individual words in an artificial way. Ideally, however, sound and rhythm must be considered in conjunction with the syntagms and words which produce them, since it is just this meeting and exchange between sound and meaning in the context of the line that gives poetry its life.

FORM: BALLAD, SONNET OR CANZONE?

These were by far the three forms most commonly adopted by *Duecento* poets. According to Dante, who wrote in detail on such questions in *De vulgari eloquentia*, the canzone was considered to be the noblest form and therefore that most suited to serious themes, such as the discussion of the nature of love. Its length, which generally consisted of between five and seven stanzas, was greater than any other form and allowed for the development of an argument. Indeed, in some ways, it resembled a school essay in structure: an opening stanza introduced the theme, then there were three or four stanzas each dealing with a separate aspect of the subject at hand, and, finally, the poet fashioned a neat conclusion.

The number of lines in a stanza was not fixed, but each stanza within a canzone had to have an identical structure. The stanza was divided into two parts, a *fronte* (divided into two identical *piedi* or feet), and a *sirima* (sometimes divided into two identical *volte*). The canzone often concluded with a *congedo*, a leave taking, which could be identical to one of the previous stanzas in structure, or to the *sirima* of those stanzas.

Dante was a master of the canzone, and produced many fine examples. Cavalcanti, on the other hand, is survived by only two: 'Io non pensavo che lo cor giammai' and the *tour de force* 'Donna me prega'.[9] In part we might presume this surprising fact to be due to impatience on Cavalcanti's part with the length of the canzone. The sonnet and isolated stanza are more concise forms, and were suited therefore to generating the restless and claustrophobic atmosphere which is a feature of many compositions. Moreover, Cavalcanti was an innovator. For the first time, features associated with the canzone, such as the *congedo* and the serious discussion of love, were incorporated by Guido into the sonnet and the ballad.

While the canzone had had a long history in Provençal lyric traditions before arriving in Italy around 1230, the sonnet is said to be the invention of Giacomo da

Lentini. At least in origin, it is really a single stanza from a canzone, having the same internal structure of two *piedi* (the quatrains), followed by a *sirima* (the sestet). Its length (fourteen lines) did not allow for the same thematic breadth or development as the canzone. It was short and sharply focussed. It was the form favoured for *rime di corrispondenza*, but was certainly not limited to this type of poem. Dante is dismissive of the sonnet in *De vulgari eloquentia*, and most of his own efforts in this form were written during his *stilnovo* phase and before he championed the canzone. Yet the sonnet still had much to offer, as its later popularity throughout Europe testifies. It is by far the most common form in the corpus of Cavalcanti's poetry: thirty-six sonnets survive. Of these, fifteen are correspondence poems, and two are clearly early compositions. The remaining nineteen pertain to that broad thematic area which is Cavalcanti's examination of love, and particularly, love's damaging influence on the lover.

The third form commonly used by Cavalcanti is the ballad. Like the canzone its origins were linked to song, that is, a composition accompanied by music. The content of the ballad was traditionally of a lighter nature than that of the canzone because it had originally been a dance piece, which saw the opening refrain repeated after each stanza. The stanza itself was divided into two or three *mutazioni* (each of two or three lines), and a *volta* which mimicked the refrain in length and rhyme scheme. By the time of Cavalcanti, the refrain stood at the head of the poem as an introduction or summary of the content of the whole, but it is unlikely that it was repeated after every stanza.

One important aspect of the ballad (and to some extent the canzone and sonnet) that is striking for readers today concerns the thematic structure. The thematic structure of a *Duecento* ballad did not necessarily proceed in a forward linear motion. Often individual stanzas were quite independent of each other, offering a series of variations on the main theme rather than a logical progression.[10] Sometimes, as in poem 16, this means that the two stanzas appear to be set at the same moment in time, and recount different aspects of the same miraculous event. At other times, as in poem 13, the effect of this structuring aesthetic is such that, to a modern reader, individual stanzas may appear repetitive. These stanzas adopt the same key words and relate the same events or feelings. But the perspective will be slightly different, as if Guido were circling around a particular idea or emotion and taking snap-shots from various angles in order to build a more complex picture.

Due to its traditional link to dance, the ballad was not considered a form suited to the highest levels of poetry. As Dante tells us in *De vulgari eloquentia* (II,iii,5):

> *sed cantiones per se totum quod debent efficiunt, quod ballate non faciunt – indigent enim plausoribus, ad quos edite sunt: ergo cantiones nobiliores ballatis esse sequitur extimandas, et per consequens nobilissimum aliorum esse modum illarum, cum nemo dubitet quin ballate sonitus nobilitate modi excellant.*

> [but, canzoni realize themselves by themselves, a capacity that ballads do not have, since they also require dancers, for whom they were created. And so it is judged that canzoni are more noble than ballads, and as a result the metre of the canzone can be considered the most noble of all, given that no one can doubt that ballads are superior to sonnets as far as nobility of metre is concerned.]

The ballad was a form cultivated in Italy only from the middle of the *Duecento* onwards, having grown out of the Provençal *balada* or *dansa*. Cavalcanti was, in fact, one of the major promoters of the ballad. We see this in the relatively large number of ballads he wrote (eleven of the fifty-two extant poems in his corpus are ballads); significantly, he pushed the form beyond its traditional thematic restrictions. For example, in 'Veggio negli occhi della donna mia' the content is that of a *loda* or praise poem, in which the narrator's lady is praised with reverence and gravitas. At the other extreme is 'In un boschetto trova' pasturella', a ballad which recounts an amorous encounter with a shepherd girl.

RHYME

Rhyme was an important aspect in the structure of any poem from the *Duecento*. If we think about the stanza not only as a group of lines, but also as a space or 'room' within which words are arranged and echo, then it is rhyme that gives shape to that 'room'. Another way of thinking of rhyme words is as a series of musical threads that bind the stanza together. For Dante, rhyme plays an important part in the overall musical effect of a poem: 'et ex hoc maxime totius armonie dulcendo intenditur' [from these [mixed rhymes] one seeks the sweetness of a harmonic whole] (De vulgari eloquentia II, xiii, 4). By mixed rhymes, Dante means rhymes that merely have the same tonic vowel and ending, as opposed to the sestina, for example, which uses the same words in each stanza. Rhyme words were often key words for the understanding of a line. Attention is focussed on them because they come at the end of a line, and because of the echo or chime they produce with other linked rhyme words.

The rhyme scheme was generally structured to give the stanza a sense of balance and harmony. A rhyme scheme adopted in many of Cavalcanti's sonnets, for example, is ABBA ABBA CDE DCE. But Cavalcanti was not afraid to experiment with rhyme schemes. In 'L'anima mia vilment' è sbigotita' he uses an unusual and unbalanced structure ABBB BAAA CDD DCC to mirror the disarray of the narrator's sentiments.

THE LINE

The line, too, was highly structured in *Duecento* poetry. In accordance with its origins in music, the line needed to be measured, not by the number of words it contained, but by the length of time it took to be uttered. The number of syllables, although it may seem a rough form of measurement, was therefore central, and for this reason Italian verse is often described as syllabic. But the syllables within a word are not always of equal importance. Each word has a tonic stress, and the requirements of the line were such that some of the stresses had to fall in fixed places. For this reason Italian verse is best described as accentual-syllabic.

By far the most common line in Italian poetry, and that used most frequently by Cavalcanti, is the hendecasyllable, which consists of eleven syllables. At least two of these syllables have strong stresses (these are known as principal stresses). One of the stresses always fell on the tenth syllable (generally the penultimate syllable). The other could either fall on the fourth or the sixth syllable. In this way the line divided into two unequal halves, or hemistiches, with the stress marking the end of the half. A caesura, or break, is said to divide the two hemistiches and can be strong or weak, depending on whether or not the syntax of the line reflects a break. The halves are never exactly even and vary from line to line because the stress in the middle of the line is not fixed.

In the case where the principal stress (besides that at the end of the line) falls on the sixth metrically relevant syllable, the line is said to be *a maiore*, meaning that the first half of the line is larger than the second. Where a principal stress falls on the fourth metrically relevant syllable, the line is said to be *a minore*, meaning that the first half of the line is smaller than the second. In this latter case the line has a further stress on either the seventh or eighth syllable.

This arrangement allows for a structure that is remarkably flexible and varied. It is vary rare for two consecutive lines to have the same rhythm. And, of course, due to strong tonic accents in words, other stresses may also be present in the line in varying degrees beyond the two or three principal stresses. Such a metre is highly flexible, and acknowledges the infinite combination of sounds and words within a line. In his description of the hendecasyllable in *De vulgari eloquentia*, Dante advocates flexibility of position for stresses other than the tenth, and he also prefers lines of an uneven number of syllables. In such cases lines avoid monotony of stress position: 'Parisillabis vero propter sui ruditatem non utimur nisi raro: retinent enim naturam suorum numerorum, qui numeris imparibus quemadmodum materia forme subsistunt' [Lines of even numbers of syllables are rarely used because they are without refinement; for they retain the nature of their numbers, which are subordinate to odd numbers just as matter is to form] (*De vulgari eloquentia*, II, v, 7).

Variation within individual lines is further increased by the use of synaeresis. This means that two vowels in separate syllables, which would normally be pronounced separately, can be elided for the sake of the syllabic count. Take, for example, the following line from poem 16: 'veder mi par de la sua labbia uscire'. Where *labbia uscire* would normally be five syllables, the final syllable of the first word is elided with the opening syllable of the second word to give four syllables, and allow the line to stay within the bounds of the hendecasyllable. Given the much greater number of words that end in a vowel in Italian than is the case in English, it is easy to imagine the prevalence of this phenomenon. Another technique adopted by Cavalcanti with a similar aim in view is apocope, which refers to the shortening of words by the removal of a final or initial vowel, as witnessed in the use both of *veder* and *par* in the first hemistich of the line quoted above. In short, the hendecasyllable is a complex and subtle system for structuring the line, one which has developed organically out of the intrinsic qualities of the Italian language itself.

CHAPTER 3. *È TANT' E DRITTA E SIMIGLIANTE COSA*: CAVALCANTI IN ENGLISH

A NOTE ON THE PRESENT TRANSLATIONS

Dante is, of course, correct: poetry is impossible to translate. And yet translation needs to happen if cultures are to renew themselves and remain vibrant. How does one translate a poem, then? To answer this we need a cursory definition of poetry.

Poetry involves language; but language in a heightened state of self-awareness. A tension arises in a poem in large part from the way words have two sides: there is the sphere of meaning a word has within a language system, and there is its physical nature, a sign on the page and a shape in our mouths. Poetry forces words to enact both sides of their being similtaneously, and possibly in different ways.

Sound and sense. These two elements of language are always in dialogue in a poem and can never be at rest. This has important implications for the translator. While the prose translation of a poetic text focusses on the sense, the poetic translation recognises that finding an equivalent for the original on a semantic level is only one part of the job. It is equally important to carry over the way the original words work as sound, and the way sound and sense interact. Of course, sound itself is a term which one needs to consider on various levels, especially if we adopt it to encompass those aspects that contribute to the physicality of language. It is most obviously the vibrations that are produced when we enunciate words. It is alliteration and other phonetic echoes that link words in ways other than syntax. But because the word is also a physical sign on the page, visual and etymological links can also be important. On a broader level sound is the metre, the rhyme, the form of the poem, its structural unity and harmony. On another level still, it is the relation between syntax and rhetoric, and between syntax and metre.

These aspects of poetry remind us that words are not static signs or concepts that pass easily from one reader to another, or from one language to another. They are physical objects, shaded and complex, elusive in their spheres of meaning, different for each of us, and tied up with our own sense of self. In drawing our attention to such a situation poetry keeps language vital and challenges our assumption that words can signify easily. Poetry, then, is in the strange position of wielding words to communicate meaning, and at the same time allowing those very words to reveal the gap between language and experience, as we find in the sestet of poem 2:

> *Non si poria contar la sua piagenza,*
> *ch'a le' s'inchin'ogni gentil vertute,*
> *e la beltate per sua dea la mostra.*
>
> *Non fu sì alta già la mente nostra*
> *e non si pose 'n noi tanta salute,*
> *che propiamente n'aviàn canoscenza.*

This tension is essential to poetry, and it needs to be kept in mind by the translator.

I started by agreeing with Dante's claim that poetry cannot be translated. The brief discussion of sound and the physicality of language would seem to limit that possibility even further. But these aspects of poetry remind us that, as readers, we come to a poem not as to a text so much as to a process of engaging with the possibilities of language. As Mallarmé says, 'La Poésie est l'espression, par le langage humain ramené à son rythme essentiel, du sens mystérieux des aspects de l'existence: elle doue ainsi d'authenticité notre séjour et constitue la seule tâche spirituelle'. [Poetry is the expression of the mysterious sense of aspects of existence by means of human language pushed to its essential rhythm. Thus poetry authenticates our existence and constitutes our sole spiritual task.][11] To recognize this is to understand the limits of translation (its impossibility, if you like, because the translation will ever take the place of the original), but also its potential. Poetry can be recreated by making the translation a new poem in English with a life-force of its own.

Whether this has been achieved or not is left to the reader's judgement. The play within a line between syntax and rhetoric, and particularly those aspects of repetition so common in poetry, such as alliteration and assonance, are not guided by fixed rules, and their effect on the whole is impossible to calibrate. There is no bilingual dictionary of poetic tricks to help the translator.

Aspects of poetry that may be considered on a more concrete level are those of metre and rhyme. A question that faces any translator of poetry written in a formal metre is to what extent constraints such as rhyme and metre should be imitated. Firstly, let us look at metre. We described the hendecasyllable in the previous chapter as a complex and flexible system for structuring a line of verse, one which has evolved out of the Italian language itself. These points are important to keep in mind when one turns to translation. The traditional view that the English iambic pentameter is the best equivalent for the Italian hendecasyllable is not always correct. It may have a similar pre-eminence in English language poetry to the hendecasyllable, but on a material level the iambic pentameter, with it's five fixed feet, is very different to the rhythmic variety of the hendecasyllable. Often, for example, an English tetrameter comes closer to the length and weight of a hendecasyllable by Cavalcanti, and avoids the need for padding. On the whole, however, I have structured the lines of the translations around a loose iambic rhythm of four or five feet.

Rhyme is an important element in the poetry of Cavalcanti. Should it be maintained? Ideally, yes. But rhyme in contemporary English language poetry has a very complex set of cultural assumptions behind it. With the odd exception, rhyme was considered essential in lyric poetry from at least the fifteenth century through to the the end of the nineteenth century. But in the last 100 years the importance of rhyme in a poem has changed: today rhyme may sound old-fasioned, or it may indicate the playful spirit of a poet inspired by the *Oulipo*, or it could stand anywhere in between. It is naive to presume that use of rhyme automatically enables one to come closer to the original. Just as there are many types of English, so too there are many ways of using rhyme.

To ignore rhyme and the part it plays in a poem by Cavalcanti seems equally dangerous. My own approach has been something of a compromise. In many of the translations that follow I have used fragments of rhyme. Sometimes full rhyme, sometimes assonance. Sometimes following the rhyme pattern of the original closely, sometimes altering it. In a few cases, such as poem 18 'Donna me prega', I have made no use of rhyme, instead an iambic rhythm is the main formal element. But the translations taken as a whole negotiate a balance between the importance of rhyme to the original and the new relationship between form and content of the poem in English. Fragments, like the ruins of the Roman forum, suggest to the imagination what once existed but also that which has suffered a change through time and language, never to be fully restored. Fragments acknowledge both the ideal original state and the impossibility of recreating that original perfectly. These translations do not eschew rhyme altogether, pretending it played no part in the original. But they do not attempt to recreate a rhyme pattern perfectly, for that only comes at the exclusion of other elements of equal importance. This might seem a rather haphazard approach. Fragments, after all, suggest something incomplete. But it is important to remember that translations themselves, by their very nature, are imperfect artefacts that require the imagination of the reader to be perfectly realised, just as they will always require the original to be valid and complete.

What we see of the Roman Forum today is evocative, but ultimately leaves us wishing for maps, guides and models of how it might once have been. It is my hope that these versions of Cavalcanti may be a fragmentary guide to this fascinating poet. They do not aim to replace the original or other English versions, but rather to exist in dialogue with other Cavalcantis. To this end, each poem is accompanied by a short introduction and detailed annotations. This material can help to contextualise a medieval poem for a modern English-speaking audience, identify contentious points of interpretation, and, at critical points, offer alternative English versions with which the present version can be compared. In this way the annotations trace the process of translating the poem, and allow the reader to engage in the dialogue between languages and cultures that is part of all translation. They offer a map that anchors the recreation more firmly to the original.

A further map is offered to readers in the remainder of this chapter, where two important English verse translators are examined in detail, Dante Gabriel Rossetti and Ezra Pound. What follows aims to give a wider critical perspective on the translation process and the assumptions the translator brings to his or her activity. Eventually readers may also bring some of these ideas to bear on the current versions.

DANTE GABRIEL ROSSETTI: POSSESSIONS OF BEAUTY

Dante Gabriel Rossetti is best known as a Pre-Raphaelite painter and poet, but his importance rests also on his work as a translator.[12] In 1861, at the age of 33, Rossetti published a monumental work of translation, *The Early Italian Poets*. It included not only one of the first English versions of Dante's *Vita Nuova* and selected lyric poetry, but the first anthology of Italian vernacular poetry of the *Duecento* in English. In all over fifty-nine poets were translated into English verse of a consistently high standard, with Cavalcanti's poems given a prominence only second to those of Dante.

Rossetti's publication coincided with a growing interest in Italian literature in England in the first half of the nineteenth century. In part this interest was due to the success of Henry Francis Cary's translation of the *Commedia*, first published as a whole in 1814 (*Inferno* had appeared in 1805). Previously, Dante and Italian medieval literature in general were little known in England. English interest in Italy in the eighteenth century had found expression in the Grand Tour, a pilgrimage to ancient cultural sites, as well as to the new expressions of classical culture in Renaissance Italy. Ariosto's *Orlando furioso*, for example, had already been translated fully three times before the first English version of the *Commedia* by Henry Boyd came out in 1802.

Cary's Dante in blank verse proved more lasting than Boyd's, and met with the approval of Ugo Foscolo, who had arrived in London as a political refugee in

1816, going on to become an instrumental figure in raising the profile of Italian literature in his adopted home.[13] Another Italian who followed a similar path was Rossetti's own father, Gabriele Rossetti (1783-1854), who came to England in 1824 as a political exile and became a celebrated but controversial Dante scholar.

Two other publications should be recorded as part of this growing interest in Dante and medieval Italy. The first is Carlyle's *On Heroes, Hero Worship and the Heroic in History*, published in 1841. In the lecture entitled 'The Hero as Poet' Shakespeare was paired with Dante. The second is Browning's publication in 1840 of *Sordello*, which follows the synonymous troubadour through twelfth and thirteenth century Italy, and from which Rossetti quotes a passage in his Preface to *The Early Italian Poets*.

So while *The Early Italian Poets* was the first comprehensive anthology of the vernacular poets of the *Duecento* in English, it grew out of a boom in interest in such literature over the previous fifty years. The volume was divided into two parts. 'Part I: Poets chiefly before Dante' contained extracts from the work of forty-four poets, ranging from the main members of the Sicilian School through to Guinizzelli, by way of Guittone; later poets such as Franco Sacchetti and Fazio degli Uberti were also included. Many of the poets are represented by a single composition. The ordering is chaotic by modern standards. Guinizzelli comes in the middle of representatives of the Sicilian School, and Guittone, represented by a single sonnet, is located immediately after Giacomino Pugliese.

'Part II: Dante and his Circle' is more focused. It contains fourteen poets, though it centres on Dante and Cavalcanti, who open the section. Dante has fourteen poems in addition to the *Vita Nuova*. Cavalcanti has twenty-three compositions, while Cino da Pistoia is represented by fourteen poems.

In 1874 Rossetti reissued the book under the title *Dante and his Circle*. The main difference from the earlier edition was the change in ordering. Parts I and II were inverted, so that the volume opened with Dante and Cavalcanti, before moving on to the earlier poetry. Minor changes were made to a few translations. The selection from Cavalcanti remained unaltered in ordering and untouched by textual revision.[14]

In his admiration of Dante and Cavalcanti Rossetti seems to take after Carlyle for whom 'universal history, the history of what man has accomplished in this world, is at bottom the History of Great Men'.[15] Dante is clearly at the centre of this circle of creativity, but Cavalcanti is in close orbit, with considerable space dedicated to describing his biography in the preface. *The Early Italian Poets* was one manifestation of Rossetti's project in this direction; he was also attempting to make mythic heroes of Dante and his circle in his visual art of the same period. It is worth remembering that Rossetti had changed his name from Gabriel Charles Dante to Dante Gabriel in his twenties, perhaps as part of that process of self-identification with the earlier Italian poet which was to remain with him for much of his life, proving a source of inspiration for both his poetry and his visual art.

If Dante was the main hero for Rossetti, Cavalcanti was something of a flawed model. On the one hand, Rossetti described him as being 'distinguished by great personal beauty, high accomplishments of all kinds, and daring nobility of soul'. Yet on the other hand Rossetti could write:

> Self-reliant pride gave its colour to all his moods; making his exploits as a soldier frequently abortive through headstrong ardour of partisanship, and causing the perversity of a logician to prevail in much of his amorous poetry. The writings of his contemporaries, as well as much of his own, tend to show him rash in war, fickle in love, and presumptuous in belief.[16]

This censure of Cavalcanti's character also finds expression in the choice of poems translated. Rossetti translates twenty-three poems by Cavalcanti.[17] This is a significant amount in the context of *The Early Italian Poets*. We are led to expect a representative selection, but, unfortunately, this is not the case. Of the twenty-three translations, eleven are correspondence sonnets, including the five addressed specifically to Dante. Rossetti includes three early praise sonnets (including poems 1 and 2), but none of the more mature praise poems such as 15 and 16. The licentious vein of Cavalcanti's corpus is well represented, with the Toulousan sonnet, the ballad to the two 'foresette' and the *Pasturella* ballad (poems 19, 20 and 21). Poem 22 is also represented, though the title 'In Exile at Sarzana' is inaccurate. It is surprising that only five compositions represent what is the major theme in the corpus, that of the destructive nature of love and the narrator's suffering as a result. These are poem 12, 'O tu, che porti nelli occhi sovente', 'La forte e nova mia disaventura', 'S'io prego questa donna che Pietate', and a *stanza isolata*, 'Se m'ha del tutto oblïato Merzede', which Rossetti calls a 'ballata'.

The result is a rather skewed representation that favours the lighter tone of the correspondence sonnets, to the detriment of more tragic and original examinations of the metaphysics of love for which Cavalcanti is famous today. Rossetti's attitude is most clearly evident in his decision not to translate the famous canzone 'Donna me prega'. He writes of it:

> A love-song which acts as such a fly-catcher for priests and pedants looks very suspicious; and accordingly, on examination, it proves to be a poem beside the purpose of poetry, filled with metaphysical jargon, and perhaps the very worst of Guido's productions. [...] I have not translated it, as being of little true interest (Introduction, 14-15).

The general preface to *The Early Italian Poets* is the principal source of information for Rossetti's ideas on the translation of poetry. He describes his versions as 'rhythmical translation'. The rhymed or poetic translation rests on a concept which Rossetti calls 'beauty':

> The only true motive for putting poetry into a fresh language must be to endow a fresh nation, as far as possible, with one more possession of beauty. Poetry not being an exact science, literality of rendering is altogether secondary to this chief law. I say *literality*, – not fidelity, which is by no means the same thing. When literality can be combined with what is thus the primary condition of success, the translator is fortunate, and must strive his utmost to unite them; when such object can only be obtained by paraphrase, that is his only path (Preface, xiii).

Fidelity to the original is Rossetti's aim. But this fidelity is not primarily concerned with 'literality', so much as the beauty of the original. 'Beauty', then, is the key to success, though Rossetti makes no attempt to define it. Such is the importance of capturing this beauty of the original that it may require paraphrase. The use of the word paraphrase is ambivalent. I shall attempt to exemplify what it may have entailed in the case of Cavalcanti later.

While 'beauty' is not defined by the poet, a look at the translations themselves reveals that maintaining the form and rhyme scheme of the original, and the use of an iambic pentameter line, were important elements. There is no question that in

Rossetti's versions such elements of form and metre survive the passage from Italian to English unscathed. Rossetti subtitled his book 'A Collection of Lyrics Translated in the Original Metre'. The general consensus in nineteenth century England was that the iambic pentameter line reflected the Italian hendecasyllable. The iambic pentameter was the line of Shakespeare and Milton. It was also the line adopted by Cary for his translation of Dante, leading Foscolo to state that 'if Dante had written in English that is the form he would have chosen'.[18]

Rossetti has a tendency to use padding to maintain the metre of individual lines. A good example can be seen in his version of poem 1 (which in *The Early Italian Poets* became 'III. Sonnet. He compares all Things with his Lady, and finds them wanting'). This early praise poem conforms to the genre known as a *plazer*, in which the poet lists a series of images of beauty, all of which are found to pale in comparison with the beauty of the poet's lady in the sestet. Here is Rossetti's translation:

> Beauty in woman; the high will's decree;
> Fair knighthood arm'd for manly exercise;
> The pleasant song of birds; love's soft replies;
> The strength of rapid ships upon the sea;
> The serene air when light begins to be;
> The white snow, without wind that falls and lies;
> Fields of flower; the place where waters rise;
> Silver and gold; azure in jewellery:–
> Weigh'd against these, the sweet and quiet worth
> Which my dear lady cherishes at heart
> Might seem a little matter to be shown;
> Being truly, over these, as much apart
> As the whole heaven is greater than this earth.
> All good to kindred natures cleaveth soon.

Line 3 of Rossetti's version is worth looking at in detail. Neither 'pleasant' nor 'soft' appears in Cavalcanti ('cantar d'augelli e ragionar d'amore'), and, indeed, neither adjective serves to clarify or render more precise the description, which reads literally as, 'the singing of birds, and the reasoning of love'. These adjectives fill out the ten syllables of the iambic pentameter line. If this were all they did we might consider them to be harmless. But, whereas Cavalcanti's line is characterised by a clarity and simplicity of image, Rossetti's adjectives contribute a vagueness which has much to do with the spirit of his own poetry but very little in common with that of Cavalcanti. Calvino, in *Lezioni americane*, praised this sonnet for its quality of lightness, *leggerezza*' (Calvino 19). Rossetti's adjectives weigh his translation down, and remind us that the trouble with padding is that it is never simply an appendage, but an altering of the very fabric of the poetry.

At times padding is required for the sake of the rhyme scheme. In line 5 of the same sonnet, for example, Rossetti has resorted to the unhappy expression 'when light begins to be', and in line 6 the beautiful original, 'e bianca neve scender senza venti', is made clumsy in the English poet's version: 'The white snow, without wind that falls and lies'. Rossetti alters the syntax so that the wind appears to be a missing attribute of the snow itself, and adds the pleonastic 'lies' in order to accommodate the rhyme.

Padding examined on a line to line basis is hard to justify. At a structural level, however, things change. The uniformity of the original has been maintained by the use of regular metre and rhyme scheme. In general the iambic pentameter line in these translations is managed with skill, without overly distorting the syntax of phrases, and while containing just enough variation in the first feet to offer relief from monotony. The qualities of clarity and lightness in the original do come across in Rossetti's command of the iambic pentameter, together with the fluid syntax. This combination of syntax and metre in Rossetti reflects the original well in the first quatrain, for example. Lines 1 and 3 follow Cavalcanti in that each hemistich is a complete syntactical unit, while lines 2 and 4 are each made up of a single syntagm.

Some imprecision at the semantic level does exist. In line 1, for example, it is hard to know what Rossetti means by 'the high will's decree'; and how does it correspond to 'e di saccente core'? A literal translation of the first line might read, 'Beauty in women, and wisdom of heart'. Possibly 'high will' is meant as a circumlocution for 'reason', but it remains obscure. In line 2 'manly' is misleading for 'genti', meaning 'gentile' or 'noble in spirit'.

To be fair, this particular sonnet offers many unusual difficulties to the translator due to its stylised language. Line 7, for example, 'rivera d'acqua e prato d'ogni fiore' is almost impossible to bring alive as poetry. A literal version might run, 'river of water, and field with every flower'. This is not very inspiring stuff, and Rossetti does well to emphasise the musical attributes of his line – the alliteration in the first hemistich, the pleasant progression of vowel sounds in the second.

Beyond form and metre, such musical qualities as alliteration would seem to play a part in Rossetti's concept of beauty. Andrea Zanzotto identifies elements such as rhythm, sound, figures of repetition such as alliteration and rhyme, for example, as contributing to the physicality of language. These aspects of language remind us of the medium's spoken nature, and affect us at the level of sensation. As Zanzotto describes, they occur in the most unknown movements of the body of the speaker, 'attraverso i movimenti più incogniti del corpo del parlante'.[19] As a result, it is not easy to identify exactly how they work in the original and how they should be translated. They form that 'legame musaico armonizzata' which, according to Dante, made the translation of poetry impossible (*Convivio* I, vii, 14). As with metre, however, so too with music: if the exact effect of individual rhythms and sounds within a line cannot often be repeated in the target language, at the level of the poem as a whole, similar techniques can be adopted by the translator. Where they are present they seem to give a certain necessity or authority to a line of verse, as in line 6 of Rossetti, 'The white snow, without wind that falls and lies'. Syntactically awkward perhaps, compared to the original, but without doubt a strong line due to the alliteration of 'w', and the repeated vowel sounds.

So far I have examined how Rossetti modifies the semantic or literal level of the poem in order to give priority to aspects of form, metre, and sound. In all these situations one find example of what Rossetti had termed paraphrase. In the sonnet in question, however, a modification of the attributes of the narrator's lady takes place, suggesting that creating 'a possession of beauty' also requires paraphrase at the level of content. This can best be seen by looking at the sestet as a whole. For Cavalcanti the lady represents an ideal unison of physical beauty, nobility of heart, and spiritual knowledge, as he makes clear in lines 9 and 10, 'la beltate e la valenza / de la mia donna e 'l su' gentil coraggio', and again in line 12, 'e tanto più d'ogn'altr' ha canoscenza'. These attributes have been reduced by Rossetti to the single expression, 'sweet and quiet worth' in line 9, while the other attributes of lines 10 and 12 have been lost in the change in syntactical structure.

Another example of paraphrase at the level of content occurs in Rossetti's version of poem 22. The original contains one of Cavalcanti's favourite terms, *spirito*. Yet the word appears on only three occasions in the poems selected by

Rossetti (poem 20, poem 22 and 'La forte e nova mia disaventura'), again revealing his one-sided representation, since the spirits tend to be connected with those poems where Cavalcanti is describing the destructive nature of love. In lines 19 and 20 of poem 22 Cavalcanti writes, '[...] 'l cor si sbatte forte / per quel che ciascun spirito ragiona'. Rossetti has, '[...] my heart still travaileth / Through the sore pangs which in my soul are bred'. The spirits have become pangs, and whereas they were personified in the original and had the ability to speak, they are now a physical reaction in the soul. Pangs, of course, would need no explanation for Rossetti's audience, while a term like *spirito* was likely to be misunderstood without some explanation. But the flavour of the original has changed.

Such a transformation at what we might call the level of object or symbol, as opposed to transformations at the level of word, is a common practice in translation, especially when moving between radically different cultures. André Lefevere, in his book *Translating Poetry: Seven Strategies and a Blueprint*, gives this aspect of translation the acronym tpt (time, place, and tradition). By this, he means those elements in a text which 'are very closely linked to the time, place, and tradition in which that source text was written, and have, therefore, become difficult, if not impossible to understand and appreciate fully in a different tpt'.[20] The approach adopted in my edition of Cavalcanti is to cover this ground in the introduction and notes to the poems. Lefevere argued that such editorial intervention takes away the independence of the poem, its ability to stand alone as a work of art. The solution, according to Lefevere, is to find equivalent symbols or signs in the target culture. Rossetti would probably have agreed. His insistence that the translation had to work as a poem in the target language, had to offer 'one more possession of beauty' suggests that he cherished a similar freedom from editorial scaffolding. The transformation of the lady and the spirits in the poems above might be considered in this light.

Such a method of translation is closer to the kind of poetic translation known as imitation. This approach is valid in itself, but the resulting version does stray somewhat from what Rossetti himself leads us to expect from his translations when, in the Preface, he describes, perhaps somewhat naively, his desire 'to give a full and truthful view of early Italian poetry'. Indeed later he suggests that 'the task of the translator (and with all humility be it spoken) is one of some self-denial. Often would he avail himself of any special grace of his own idiom and epoch, if his will belonged to him' (xiv).

It seems evident, given Rossetti's attention to formal aspects of poetry, that he recognised the necessity of maintaining a unity between form and content. There are examples of paraphrase in these versions of Cavalcanti, alterations which from our own perspective appear to alter the original unjustly. On the whole, however, they are isolated examples. Rossetti was not a radical translator. His aim was always to combine fidelity to the poem's beauty with what he termed 'literality'. In this sense his understanding of the term 'paraphrase' is similar to that of Dryden, for whom it designates a middle ground between the extremes of word-for-word literalism on the one hand, and freedom of imitation on the other – a middle ground where 'the author is kept in view by the translator, so as never to be lost, but his words are not so strongly followed as his sense'.[21]

EZRA POUND: FIDELITY AND THE MASCULINE SPIRIT

For Ezra Pound the translation of poetry and the writing of original verse were closely linked activities. Both aimed to invigorate languages and the cultures that spoke through them. Pound translated and adapted from a range of languages, and the results were often intermingled with his original verse, from the early collection, *Personae* (1909), through to the *Cantos*. Like his appropriation of the voices of other writers in dramatic monologues, translating, for Pound, was a form of donning a mask. It was a fusing of the translator's own spirit with the spirit of the poem to be rendered. As T. S. Eliot said in his 'Introduction' to Pound's *Selected Poems* in 1948, 'Good translation is not merely translation, for the translator is giving the original through himself, and finding himself through the original'.

Pound's experience of translating Guido Cavalcanti exemplifies this fusion extremely well. He grappled with the persona of Cavalcanti for more than three decades. As early as 1910 his first version of the sonnet 'Chi è questa' was published in the volume *Provença*. A series of translations led to *The Sonnets and Ballate of Guido Cavalcanti* in 1912. In 1932 Pound composed an opera entitled *Cavalcanti*, with a libretto based on poems by Cavalcanti and Sordello, and as late as 1944 he wrote Cantos LXXII and LXXIII in Italian as dramatic monologues in the voice of the Tuscan poet. During this period Pound worked on Cavalcanti not only as a poet, however, but also as a scholar. He produced a critical edition of the Italian originals in 1932, *Guido Cavalcanti Rime, edizione rappezzata fra le rovine*, and wrote three essays on Cavalcanti published in *The Dial*. These were later united into the essay 'Cavalcanti' in *Make It New* (1934).[22] This twofold approach to the medieval poet distinguishes Pound's work on Cavalcanti from his dealings with other writers and makes the versions themselves difficult to place. Comments Pound himself made about his versions of Cavalcanti, and his repeated returns to Cavalcanti in different guises and genres, suggest just such an ambiguity, as he stresses at one point the primacy of conveying accuracy of meaning, at the next the importance of rhythm and sound as carriers of Cavalcanti's spirit.[23]

The epigraph to *Personae*, published when Pound was twenty-four years old, reads 'Make-strong old dreams lest this our world lose heart'. This phrase fittingly embodies two of the most striking elements in the pre-Imagist Pound: firstly a nineteenth century diction, often termed Wardour Street language, and, secondly, his obsession with the past, and particularly that period of the thirteenth century which saw the rise of vernacular poetry in France and Italy. Sustaining old dreams, for Pound, meant producing translations and poetic imitations, and writing dramatic monologues in the voices of past poets. *Personae*, for example, included such poems as 'Cino' written in the voice of Cino da Pistoia, and 'Sestina: Altaforte', which adopted that of Betrans de Born. Indeed, the concept of the persona, or mask, which Pound adopted in each poem embodies this deliberate process, and gave expression to what Louis Martz described as Pound's 'remarkable mimetic genius, his ability to absorb the style, manner and meaning of another poet, and then to interpret and recreate that role, in translations, creative adaptation, or in original poems'.[24] In 'Histrion', for example, from his second volume *A Quinzaine for This Yule*, Pound presumes to channel the past masters through his own pen in a sort of temporary metempsychosis:

> No man hath dared to write this thing as yet,
> And yet I know, how that the souls of all men great
> At times pass through us,
> And we are melted into them, and are not
> Save reflections of their souls.
> Thus am I Dante for a space and am
> One François Villon, ballad-lord and thief.

Pound's interest in the persona of Cavalcanti became evident with the publication of his fifth volume of poetry, *Canzoni* (1911),[25] where one finds a sonnet entitled 'To Guido Cavalcanti', beginning:

> Dante and I are come to learn of thee,
> Ser Guido of Florence, master of us all,
> Love, who hath set his hand upon us three,
> Bidding us twain upon thy glory call.

This poem reveals a desire for complete identification with the two early poets, as if the six centuries that separated Pound from 'Ser Guido of Florence' could be erased in the poetic act.

The Wardour Street diction of Pound's writing suggests a strong debt to Swinburne and the Pre-Raphaelites, particularly Dante Gabriel Rossetti. The anxiety of influence Pound felt in relation to this second figure perhaps help to explain his publication of *The Sonnets and Ballate of Guido Cavalcanti*, just fifty years after Rossetti's anthology *The Early Italian Poets*. Pound's book contained thirty-five sonnets and fifteen *canzoni* and ballads, that is, the majority of Cavalcanti's known corpus, all rendered into English in poetic translations. Importantly this was a bilingual edition with a considerable introduction by Pound. In this fashion Pound distanced himself from Rossetti's earlier versions of Cavalcanti, not only by providing a greater selection of poems, but in having his translations in constant relation to the originals, and also by providing a contextual and critical framework of sorts.

For Pound, as for Rossetti, translations had to be poems in themselves in order to capture the spirit of the original, but Pound also hoped that his translations would send the reader back to the original, rather than act as a substitute. Furthermore, the reader of the translation would need to be aware of the foreignness of the original. This seems to be what Pound had in mind when, in he wrote in the introduction:

> It is conceivable the poetry of a far-off time and place requires a translation not only of word and spirit but of 'accompaniment', that is, that the modern audience must in some measure be made aware of the mental content of the older audience, and of what these others drew from certain fashions of thought and speech. Six centuries of derivative

convention and loose usage have obscured the exact significances of such phrases as: 'The death of the heart', and 'The departure of the soul'.

Pound went on to describe some instances of misinterpretation by Rossetti, followed by a few pages of biographical information about Cavalcanti, and the use of terms such as *anima*, *morte*, *gentile* and *mente*. Finally, in the last two pages Pound turned to questions concerning his method of translation. He wrote,

> As for the verse itself: I believe in an ultimate and absolute rhythm … the perception of the intellect is given in the word, that of the emotions in the cadence. It is only, then, in perfect rhythm joined to the perfect word that the two-fold vision can be recorded. I have in my translations tried to bring over the qualities of Guido's rhythm, not line by line, but to embody in the whole of my English some trace of that power which implies the man.

This last phrase is typical of Pound's prose for its sweeping generalisations. There is no analysis of what exactly 'Guido's rhythm' might be, nor is there a description of how he has embodied that rhythm in the whole of his own verse. One is led to presume that there has been another metempsychosis, and that the soul of Cavalcanti, like those of Villon and Dante earlier, has passed through the young American poet. At the same time, the ambitious aim of combining the perfect rhythm and the perfect word describes the synthesis that Pound sought between fidelity to the meaning of Cavalcanti's words and to his poetic spirit.

Shortly after publication, however, Pound wrote a letter to the *Times Literary Supplement* in which he defended his method of translation against criticisms in a review that had found Pound's versions lacking in prettiness and metrical aptitude when compared to those of Rossetti. Pound's defence seems to contradict his statement about 'absolute rhythm' in the introduction:

> Guido cared more for sense than for music, and I saw fit to emphasise this essential aspect of his work. The music is easily available for anyone who will learn Italian pronunciation. The meaning is more than once in doubt even after long study. I thought I served my audience best by setting forth the meaning.[26]

Here, Pound suggests that, as a translator, he is not primarily a poet, ready to alter the original to create a new poem, but rather a scholar ready to sacrifice prettiness to accuracy.

One of Pound's last and most substantial publications directly concerned with Guido is his essay 'Cavalcanti' published in 1934.[27] Here Pound reflects on his earlier translations with some critical distance:

> When I 'translated' Guido eighteen years ago I did not see Guido at all. I saw that Rossetti had made a remarkable translation of the *Vita Nuova*, in some places improving (or at least enriching) the original; that he was indubitably the man 'sent', or 'chosen' for that particular job, and that there was something in Guido that escaped him or that was, at any rate, absent from his translations. A *robustezza*, a masculinity.

Once again, it is interesting that Pound saw his translations in relation to the earlier versions by Rossetti, and clearly felt a need to justify the presence of his own. Pound claimed to have the advantage of semantic fidelity, but equally, to have captured more of the masculine spirit of Guido, or what he had called in the 1912 introduction 'that power which implies the man'. But for Pound there was certainly a tension in this dual aim. It comes out in his reply to the reviewer above. It can best be seen in the fact that Pound returned to his translations of Cavalcanti repeatedly over the space of at least twenty years. One particular sonnet, poem 2, 'Chi è questa che vèn', exists in four distinct versions, and offers an excellent window into thinking about the difficulties Pound faced and the ways he tried to overcome them at various stages.

Pound's earliest version of 'Chi è questa che vèn' was an unpublished translation dated 1910, one of ten sonnets in a folder entitled 'Cavalcanti Sonnets' that would contribute to *The Sonnets and Ballate of Guido Cavalcanti* two years later. It is an unrhymed version in iambic pentameter in fifteen lines (line 6 in the original has been broken into two short lines by Pound for no apparent reason).

> Who is she coming, whom all gaze upon,
> Who makes the whole air tremulous with light,
> And leadeth with her Love, so no man hath

Power of speech, but each one sigheth?
Ah God! the thing she's like when her eyes turn,
Let Amor [speak it]
tell! Tis past mine utterance:
And so she seems mistress of modesty
That every other woman is named 'Wrath'.
Her charm could never be a thing to tell
For all the noble powers lean toward her.
Beauty displays her for an holy sign.
Our daring ne'er before did look so high;
But ye! there is not in you so much grace
That we can understand her rightfully.

This version follows the semantic content of the original quite closely. Indeed it seems to be a version principally concerned with carrying across the word for word meaning of Cavalcanti. The language is heavily steeped in Wardour Street, however, and this nineteenth-century spirit does flow over into changes to the content of the original in places, such as the use of the second person singular vocative in the penultimate line to replace the first person plural pronoun 'noi'.

The same year Pound published *Provença*, which contained 'Sonnet: Chi è questa':

Who is she coming, that the roses bend
Their shameless heads to do her passing honour?
Who is she coming with a light upon her
Not born of suns that with the day's end end?
Say, is it Love who hath chosen the nobler part?
Say, is it Love, that was divinity,
Who hath left his godhead that his home might be
The shameless rose of her unclouded heart?

If this be Love, where hath he won such grace?
If this be Love, how is the evil wrought,
That all men write against his darkened name?
If this be Love, if this ...

                                        O mind give place!

What holy mystery e'er was noosed in thought?
Own that thou scan'st her not, nor count it shame!

Clearly this version is an imitation of Cavalcanti's sonnet. Scholarly accuracy is not a priority. The addition of 'evil' and 'darkened name' in lines 10 and 11 suggests new spheres of meaning, as does the phrase 'the roses bend their shameless heads'. Importantly, Pound adds rhetorical elements such as anaphora and antanaclasis to give the poem a new impetus. The repetition is particularly insistent. Together with the ellipsis in line 12, this rhetorical device suggests a certain impatience, a certain forcefulness or *robustezza*.

Pound's third version appeared two years later in *The Sonnets and Ballate of Guido Cavalcanti*:

Who is she coming, drawing all men's gaze,
Who makes the air one trembling clarity
Till none can speak but each sighs piteously
Where she leads Love adown her trodden ways?

Ah God! The thing she's like when her glance strays,
Let Amor tell. 'Tis no fit speech for me.
Mistress she seems of such great modesty
That every other woman were called 'Wrath'.

No one could ever tell the charm she hath
For all the noble powers bend toward her,
She being beauty's godhead manifest.

Our daring ne'er before held such high quest
But ye! There is not in you so much grace
That we can understand her rightfully.

This is very similar to the first version. Many of the changes can be traced to a desire to implement a rhyme scheme that mimics the original ABBA ABBA CDE EDC. The results are sometimes clumsy. The C rhyme relies on the penultimate word of line 9, 'she', to rhyme with 'rightfully'. In line 1 the new version has a gerund rather than the relative clause of the first version and the original. More significantly the use of 'her glance strays' for 'gira' (literally 'turns') in line 5 changes the meaning significantly for the sake of rhyme.

Other changes suggest a desire to make this new version even more regular in its adhesion to iambic pentameter. Here the changes are linked to the presence of pseudo-archaisms. The 1910 imitation had been linguistically more uniform and gained strength as a result. Certainly, in the previous version there were archaic desinences for the verb *have*. But, in this version, expressions such as 'adown her trodden ways', 'Let Amor tell', and ''Tis no fit speech', appear to be clear lapses in a linguistic register which, on the whole, has learnt to repress its early love of Wardour Street. Anderson considers such archaisms as belonging to Pound's 'general strategy for making his readers recognise, and adjust for, the "six centuries of derivative convention and loose usage" that have blurred Cavalcanti's "exact significance"' (Anderson, xvi). But in the three phrases quoted from the sonnet above the choice of words seems to be based on a desire to smooth over the iambic rhythm of the line, rather than as a deliberate archaising technique, or as a more accurate reflection of the original. 'Adown her trodden ways' bears little resemblance to 'e mena seco', for example. It is neither a reflection of Guido's rhythm, nor of his sense. The use of such archaic expressions suggests that Pound was still struggling to exorcise the spirits of the nineteenth century in order to make way for those of the thirteenth. Indeed, as a whole, *The Sonnets and Ballate of Guido Cavalcanti* read like the first steps of an eventual journey into Modernism, as if the Italian poet were a high-priest to help Pound refine a language of his own, free of the accursed Pre-Raphaelites.

The question of how to find a suitable language for a version of a thirteenth century poet is one that must be tackled by any translator. How does one do justice to the startling linguistic energy and originality in Cavalcanti when the result of a literal translation is often a string of trite phrases such as 'my spirits are dead' or 'my heart battles hard, but feels death approach'? These are questions with which Pound battled throughout the decades in which Cavalcanti was a major presence in his work. Pound was obsessed with revitalising the spirit of Guido. Exactly what he associated with such a spirit, however, is hard to determine. Pound's work on Cavalcanti divided itself into two streams, one more scholarly, the other more creative. But in 1932 he returned specifically to the translations themselves, publishing new versions of five sonnets as part of his

Italian edition *Guido Cavalcanti Rime: Edizione rappezzata fra le rovine.* It is worth examining these mature versions to see if Pound found a language more appropriate to the medieval poet.

Comments Pound himself made in the essay 'Cavalcanti' suggest that he, at least, considered his later translations to be an advance on the earlier versions. Returning to the issue of finding a suitable language for Guido, he states that it is not a question 'of giving Guido in an English contemporary to himself' since 'the ultimate Britons were ... grunting in an idiom far more difficult for us to master than the Langue d'Oc ... or the Lingua di Si'. Rather, he writes, the translator needs to 'reach back to pre-Elizabethan English, of a period when writers were still intent on clarity and explicitness, still preferring them to magniloquence and the thundering phrase'. Again Pound's generalisations are so sweeping in nature that it is difficult to take them seriously. That only pre-Elizabethan English can achieve clarity or explicitness is a fallacy.

'Chi è questa che vèn' is one of the rewritten translations. Pound quotes it in full immediately after the above comments in the essay 'Cavalcanti' as an example of pre-Elizabethan language:

> Who is she that comes, makyng turn every man's eye
> And makyng the air to tremble with a bright clearenesse
> That leadeth with her Love, in such nearness
> No man may proffer of speech more than a sigh?
>
> Ah God, what she is like when her owne eye turneth, is
> Fit for Amor to speake, for I can not at all;
> Such is her modesty, I would call
> Every woman else but an useless uneasiness.
>
> No one could ever tell all of her pleasauntess
> In that every high noble vertu leaneth to herward,
> So Beauty sheweth her forth as her Godheade;
>
> Never before was our mind so high led
> Nor have we so much of heal as will afford
> That our thought may take her immediate in its embrace.

The first thing to note is the greater linguistic uniformity. No phrase leaps off the page as particularly out of place, except perhaps 'useless uneasiness' or 'to herward'. To my mind there is very little which situates the language specifically in the sixteenth century, apart from the orthography. Modernise the spelling and only a few expressions such as 'the air to tremble' and 'every woman else' stand out, but even they remind one more readily of the problems with Pound's 1912 version, rather than echoing Wyatt.

Again there seem to be inconsistencies with the use of archaisms. Why does Pound use 'leadeth' in line 3, but 'comes' rather than 'cometh' in line 1? In this particular case one can compare Pound's hemistich with an early seventeenth-century example. Cavalcanti's line 'Chi è questa che vèn' is an imitation of the Latin version of *Isaiah* (63,1), 'Quis est iste qui venit'. *The King James Bible* (albeit basing itself on Greek and Hebrew), in turn translates, 'Who is this that cometh'. Again the same construction in the *Song of Solomon* (3,6), 'Quae est ista quae ascendit per desertum', is rendered into English in 1611 as 'Who is this that cometh out of the wilderness'. While this is not a very rich syntagm from the point of view of the translator, it does serve to point out inconsistencies in Pound's language.

One place where the pseudo-archaic spelling plays more than a token role is in the use of 'pleasauntness' in line 9. In Pound's 1912 version this had been, 'No one could ever tell the charm she hath'. The original reads 'Non si poria contar la sua piagenza'. In adopting an archaic spelling, Pound had hoped to imbue what is a semantically poor term in standard usage with a new sense of mystery. At the same time he was able to use an English word that shared a common etymology with the original term. In this sense Pound saw the process of translation as a means of bridging that linguistic chasm produced by 'six centuries of loose usage', and reinvigorating the modern language.

But perhaps the most interesting change from the 1912 version of Cavalcanti's sonnet to the 1932 translation, is the difference in metre. Pound's earlier versions of the poem are written in a fairly strict iambic pentameter. This later version, on the other hand, is representative of the greater rhythmic freedom and range Pound achieved in the five sonnets published in 1932. The lines range from having four to six dominant stresses, and are from nine to thirteen syllables in length. While most lines have five dominant stresses, that which distinguishes them from the earlier pentameter is the range of feet. The iamb does not predominate. The result is a rhythmic flexibility reminiscent of that of the hendecasyllable.

On the whole, in the 1932 version of 'Chi è questa che vèn' Pound achieved a greater uniformity of language, coupled with a sophisticated use of rhythm and sound. The result is an authority of voice in the translation that was lacking in the earlier two versions (though not the imitation). At the same time it remains relatively accurate on a semantic level, something that cannot be said of the imitation.

But what of the so-called masculine spirit of Cavalcanti? To what extent that spirit was faithfully transmitted, or ever existed, is hard to judge given Pound's imprecise definitions of it. It seems likely that it was largely a projection of Pound's own spirit onto Guido. Perhaps such a projection was necessitated by Pound's interest in metempsychosis, or perhaps by the desire to distinguish himself and his versions from the overbearing presence of Rossetti. Pound reminds us that the translator brings just as much that is new to the translation as he or she claims to bring over from the original. Whatever the case, Pound's obsession with Cavalcanti was a fruitful source of creative stimulation. Finding a balance between semantic fidelity and that masculine spirit proved elusive to the end, as it does in any act of poetic translation, something Pound himself recognised in the concluding page of 'Cavalcanti': 'In the long run the translator is in all probability impotent to do *all* the work for the linguistically lazy reader'. With this new view of translation as an imperfect negotiation, came a greater flexibility and even fidelity in the final version of 'Chi è questa che vèn'.

NOTES

1. For a further discussion see Contini, 'Dolce stil novo' in *Poeti del Duecento* v.2 (Milan, Riccardi, 1960) pp. 443-446; and, more recently, Luciano Rossi, 'Stilnovo' in *Antologia della poesia italiana: Duecento* eds. Cesare Segre and Carlo Ossola (Turin, Einaudi, 1997) pp. 370-378.

2. Corti offers some insightful pages into Cavalcanti's renewal of the topos of death, 1978, pp. 15-18.

3. See Mario Marti, 1973, p. 157 for a discussion of personification in Cavalcanti. In the *Vita Nuova*, XXV, 7-10, personification is the rhetorical device used to demonstrate the 'maggiore licenza di parlare' [greater licence in speech] granted to poets above prose writers. Arnaut Daniel is another poet who uses personification. In 'En breu brisara 'l temps braus' he wrote 'si m'a'l sen desirs fors duich / no sap lo cors trep o'is

duoilla' [Desire has driven my senses to such extremes / I don't know whether my heart is light or heavy] (lines 35-36). Quotations from Arnaut Daniel come from *Le canzoni di Arnaut Daniel*, ed. Mario Perugi, (Milan, Ricciardi, 1979).

4. The only more frequent words are *core* (85 times), *amore* (71), *donna* (52), *dire* (61), *vedere* (60), and the equally present *morire/morte* (45). Cino da Pistoia used the word fifty-four times but his corpus is three times the length of Cavalcanti's.

5. These chapters correspond to Dante's Cavalcantian phase. For a further discussion of which see Foster and Boyde.

6. The spirits were often divided into three types: the natural spirit which had its origin and seat in the liver, and whose function was to diffuse itself through the veins and provide nourishment to the body; the vital spirit which formed in the heart and moved about the body via the arteries, and whose function was to provide energy and respiration to the body; thirdly the animal spirit, which resided in the brain, and which, via the nerves, sent messages from the senses back to the brain, whose three parts (imagination, memory and thought) it also connected.

7. 'In quello punto dico veracemente che lo spirito de la vita, lo quale dimora ne la secretissima camera de lo cuore, cominciò a tremare sì fortemente, che apparia ne li menimi polsi orribilmente.' [At that point I say truthfully that the spirit of life, which dwells in the secret room of the heart, began to tremble so violently, that it appeared terrifying in its smallest veins.] [*Vita Nuova*, II 4]

8. For a full discussion of the manuscript tradition see Contini, 1960, v. 2, pp. 899-906. The most important codices for Cavalcanti are the Chigiano L.VIII. 305 in the Biblioteca Apostolica Vaticana (mid fourteenth- century); Escurialense e. III. 23 in the Biblioteca del Escorial Madrid (fourteenth century); and the Vaticano Latino 3214 in the Biblioteca Apostolica Vaticana (compiled by Pietro Bembo in 1523).

9. The number of canzoni is sometimes given as four, but two of these, 'Poi che di doglia cor conven ch'i' porti' and Se m'ha del tutto obliato Merzede', are really *stanze isolate*, or single stanzas.

10. For a further discussion of thematic structure see Boyde, 1971, pp. 245-7.

11. Stephane Mallarmé *Correspondance. Lettres sur la poésie* (Paris, Gallimard, 1995) p. 572.

12. Rossetti's versions of Cavalcanti have received limited critical attention. See A. Paolucci, 'Ezra Pound and D. G. Rossetti as Translators of Guido Cavalcanti', *The Romanic Review*, LI 1960, 4, pp. 256-67; and E. G. Gitter, 'Rossetti's Translations of Early Italian Lyrics', *Victorian Poetry,* 1974, Vol.12, pp. 351-62. R. Edwards looks specifically at Rossetti's treatment of Guinizzelli in 'Guinizzelli's Readers and the Strategies of Historicism' quoted above. Finally, J. McGann discusses *The Early Italian Poets* in *Dante Gabriel Rossetti and the Game that Must Be Lost* (New

Haven, Yale University Press, 2000), particularly pp. 32-38; see also McGann, 'A Commentary on Some of Rossetti's Translations from Dante', *Haunted Texts, Studies in Pre-Raphaelitism in Honour of William E. Fredeman*, edited by David Latham (Toronto, University of Toronto Press, 2003) pp. 35-52.

13. 'Of all the translators of Dante with whom we are acquainted, Mr Cary is the most successful; and we cannot but consider his work as a great acquisition to the English reader'. U. Foscolo, 'Primo articolo della *Edinburgh Review*', *Studi su Dante*, parte prima, edited by G. Da Pozzo (Florence, Le Monnier, 1979) p. 42.

14. E. Gardner, editor of the Everyman edition Dante Gabriel Rossetti, *Poems and Translations* (London, J. M. Dent, 1912), follows the 1861 edition. So too does J. Marsh, editor of *Dante Gabriel Rossetti Collected Writings* (London, J. M. Dent, 1999). J. McGann, editor of *Dante Gabriel Rossetti Collected Poetry and Prose* (New Haven, Yale University Press, 2003), who prints a rather scant selection from the translations, following the order of the 1861 edition but relying on texts from that of 1874. Both the 1861 and 1874 editions can be found in *The Complete Writings and Pictures of Dante Gabriel Rossetti: A Hypermedia Research Archive*, www.rossettiarchive.org.

15. T. Carlyle, *On Heroes, Hero-Worship and the Heroic in History*, notes and introduction by M. K. Goldberg, text established by M. K. Goldberg, J. J. Brattin, and M. Engel (Berkeley, University of California Press 1993) p. 3.

16. D. G. Rossetti, 'Introduction to Part 1', *Dante and his Circle*, a new edition with preface by W. M. Rossetti (London, Ellis and Elvey, 1892) p. 6. All further references are abbreviated to Introduction and are to this edition.

17. He actually lists twenty-nine, but six of these poems are wrongly attributed to Cavalcanti. These are in Rossetti's ordering: 'V. Ballata. Of his Lady among other Ladies'; 'XII. Sonnet. On the Detection of a false Friend', which recent scholarship has almost unanimously determined to be the work of Dante (See De Robertis, pp. 223-25); and the last four *canzoni*, 'XXVI. Canzone. A Song of Fortune', 'XXVII. Canzone. A Song Against Poverty', 'XXVIII. Canzone. He laments the Presumption and Incontinence of his Youth', and 'XXIX. Canzone. A Dispute with Death'. Rossetti himself had expressed some doubt as to the authorship of these last four poems in a note to the text.

18. Cary's translation 'is executed with a fidelity almost without example; and, though the measure he has adopted, conveys no idea of the original stanza, it is perhaps the best for his purpose, and what Dante himself would have chosen, if he had written in English and in a later day' (Foscolo, p. 42).

19. Andrea Zanzotto, 'Conversazione sottovoce sul tradurre e l'essere tradotti' in *Testo a fronte*, anno V, no. 8, 1993, p. 64.

20. A. Lefevere, *Translating Poetry: Seven Strategies and a Blueprint* (Assen, Van Gorcum, 1975) pp. 84-85.

21. J. Dryden, 'Preface' to the anthology of contemporary translations of Ovid's Epistles (1680).

22. For details of all Pound's publications relating to Cavalcanti, see David Anderson, *Pound's Cavalcanti: An Edition of the Translations, Notes and Essays* (Princeton, Princeton UP, 1983). Quotes from Pound's versions and critical writing on Cavalcanti are taken from this edition.

23. The present discussion is made in the light of the book by David Anderson quoted above and his paper, 'A Language to Translate Into: The Pre-Elizabethan Idiom of Pound's Later Cavalcanti Translations', in *Studies in Medievalism*, v.II, no.I, Fall 1982. Also of interest are Lawrence Venuti, *The Translator's Invisibility* (London, Routledge, 1995); and Richard Sieburth, 'Channelling Guido: Ezra Pound's Cavalcanti Translations' in *Guido Cavalcanti tra i suoi lettori*, a cura di Maria Luisa Ardizzone (Firenze, Edizioni Cadmo, 2003).

24. Louis Martz, 'Introduction', in *Collected Early Poems of Ezra Pound*, ed. Michael J. King (London, Faber and Faber, 1977) p. xiv.

25. The titles of poems also reveal that the spirit of medieval literature which Pound was recuperating consisted not only in the voice of past masters, but also their poetic forms, for one finds original poems entitled simply, 'Canzone', or 'Sonnet in Tenzone' or 'Ballata, Fragment', mimicking the improvised titles given by editors to untitled poems by the early Italian poets, and even the imperfect way they have been preserved by posterity.

26. *Times Literary Supplement*, no. 569, December, 1912, p. 562. Quoted in Anderson, 1983, pp. xvii-iii.

27. Although the essay was published in 1934, its three parts had already been published separately in *The Dial* between 1928 and 1929.

PART 1

Early Poems

1

Biltà di donna e di saccente core,
e cavalieri armati che sien genti;
cantar d'augelli e ragionar d'amore;
adorni legni 'n mar forte correnti;

aria serena quand' apar l'albore   5
e bianca neve scender senza venti;
rivera d'acqua e prato d'ogni fiore;
oro, argento, azzuro 'n ornamenti:

ciò passa la beltate e la valenza
de la mia donna e 'l su' gentil coraggio,   10
sì che rasembra vile a chi ciò guarda;

e tanto più d'ogn'altr' ha canoscenza,
quanto lo cielo de la terra è maggio.
A simil di natura ben non tarda.

1

A lady of wisdom and highest grace,
and knights in arms when trained for chivalry,
the carols of love and songs of birds,
swift ships adorned with finest blazonry;

the sky serene when dawn appears,
and light snow falling without trace of wind,
a stream in flow through summer fields,
fine gold and lapis held in ornament;

such is surpassed by all the worth
and beauty of my lady's noble heart
and seems so paltry in comparison;

and as the sky to earth is greater
so her understanding commands all others.
To one as she all good is quick to come.

2

Chi è questa che vèn, ch'ogn'om la mira,
che fa tremar di chiaritate l'âre
e mena seco Amor, sì che parlare
null'omo pote, ma ciascun sospira?

O Deo, che sembra quando li occhi gira!   5
dical' Amor, ch'i' nol savria contare:
cotanto d'umiltà donna mi pare,
ch'ogn'altra ver' di lei i' la chiam' ira.

Non si poria contar la sua piagenza,
ch'a le' s'inchin' ogni gentil vertute,   10
e la beltate per sua dea la mostra.

Non fu sì alta già la mente nostra
e non si pose 'n noi tanta salute,
che propiamente n'aviàn canoscenza.

2

Who is she that comes, whom every man admires,
whose clarity shines through the trembling air,
who leads Love in her wake, such that where men
would speak, they can no more than sigh?

To Love I leave the charge of finding words
that tell of awe when her gaze falls on us,
humility has never taken form
as pure or true as in this lady's eye.

No human voice can hope to sound her grace,
she moves with Virtue at her side
and even Beauty holds her forth as god.

Our minds have never stretched so high before,
nor have our senses felt such joy,
that we could ever know her perfectly.

PART 2

Sonnets Addressed to Dante

3

Vedeste, al mio parere, onne valore
e tutto gioco e quanto bene om sente,
se foste in prova del segnor valente
che segnoreggia il mondo de l'onore,

poi vive in parte dove noia more,   5
e tien ragion nel cassar de la mente;
sì va soave per sonno a la gente,
che 'l cor ne porta senza far dolore.

Di voi lo core ne portò, veggendo
che vostra donn' a la morte cadea: 10
nodriala dello cor, di ciò temendo.

Quando v'apparve che se 'n gia dolendo,
fu 'l dolce sonno ch'allor si compiea,
ché 'l su' contraro lo venìa vincendo.

3

I'd say you glimpsed what is perfection,
all the worth and joy that one may feel,
if the force which took your heart was really
Love who rules in honour's dominion,

who leaves no room to know vexation,
who governs with the mind, and steals
so swiftly through your sleep you feel
no pain as your heart is carried away.

He saw your lady close to death
and took your heart in hope that he might
thereby nourish her; and when on leaving

he seemed to cry with grief the meaning
was the late hour of the night
for your sweet dream had reached the point of waning.

4

S'io fosse quelli che d'Amor fu degno,
del qual non trovo sol che rimembranza,
e la donna tenesse altra sembianza,
assai mi piaceria siffatto legno.

E tu, che se' de l'amoroso regno   5
là onde di merzé nasce speranza,
riguarda se 'l mi' spirito ha pesanza:
ch' un prest' arcier di lui ha fatto segno

e tragge l'arco, che li tese Amore,
sì lietamente, che la sua persona   10
par che di gioco porti signoria.

Or odi maraviglia ch'el disia:
lo spirito fedito li perdona,
vedendo che li strugge il suo valore.

4

Were I still deemed to be worthy by Love,
like one to whom I've no resemblance now,
and were my lady's stance more moderate,
then I would gladly sail with you, my friend.

But you who live secure in Love's reign,
where mercy from your lady nurtures hope,
consider how my own case is more bleak:
an archeress marked my spirit in her range,

and then shot home the dart which Love held out,
with such a gleeful look as seemed to say
she governed pleasure's realm capriciously.

Now hear the marvel of this mad desire:
my wounded spirit forgives her, even though
she torments and consumes our energy.

5

Dante, un sospiro messagger del core
subitamente m'assalì dormendo,
ed io mi disvegliai allor, temendo
ched e' non fosse in compagnia d'Amore.

Po' mi girai, e vidi 'l servitore   5
di monna Lagia che venìa dicendo:
"Aiutami, Pietà!", sì che piangendo
i' presi di merzé tanto valore,

ch'i' giunsi Amore ch'affilava i dardi.
Allor l'adomandai del su' tormento,   10
ed elli mi rispuose in questa guisa:

"Di' al servente che la donna è prisa,
e tengola per far su' piacimento;
e se no 'l crede, di' ch' a li occhi guardi."

5

Dante, a missive sigh escaped
my heart and struck me as I slept,
and so I started up for fear
Love might be in its company.

Then I turned to see the servant
Lady Lagia holds in love.
'Have pity, help,' he cried. Moved,
with Mercy's aid, I summoned strength

and sought Love where he sharpens darts
to ask of our friend's suffering.
He answered in the following way,

'Tell that servant the lady is caught.
I hold her for his pleasure, as one
can see by looking in her eyes.'

6

I' vegno 'l giorno a te 'nfinite volte
e tròvoti pensar troppo vilmente:
molto mi dòl della gentil tua mente
e d'assai tue vertù che ti son tolte.

Solevanti spiacer persone molte;   5
tuttor fuggivi l'annoiosa gente;
di te parlav'i', sì coralemente
che tutte le tue rime avìe ricolte.

Or non ardisco, per la vil tua vita,
far mostramento che tu' dir mi piaccia,   10
né 'n guisa vegno a te che tu mi veggi.

Se 'l presente sonetto spesso leggi,
lo spirito noioso che ti caccia
si partirà da l'anima invilita.

6

I turn to you so often in my mind
and each time dwell on just how low you've come,
and then I grieve such waste: your virtue, reason,
every noble trait now left behind.

Once you disdained these crowds, you never sought
alliance with the two-faced and malicious.
I used to speak of you with candid praise
and boldly welcomed all you wrote in rhyme.

But dare I visit you in person now,
or state the faith I have in your poetry
while you demean yourself in such a way?

Read the present sonnet over aloud
and see if that low spirit which currently
afflicts your downcast soul is driven away.

PART 3

Love as *Sbigottimento*

7

Deh, spiriti miei, quando mi vedete
con tanta pena, come non mandate
fuor della mente parole adornate
di pianto, dolorose e sbigottite?

Deh, voi vedete che 'l core ha ferite   5
di sguardo e di piacer e d'umiltate:
deh, i' vi priego che voi 'l consoliate
che son da lui le sue vertù partite.

I' veggo a luï spirito apparire
alto e gentile e di tanto valore,   10
che fa le sue vertù tutte fuggire.

Deh, i' vi priego che deggiate dire
a l'alma trista, che parl' in dolore,
com' ella fu e fie sempre d'Amore.

7

Oh, my little spirits, my life,
my will, who see me lost and stunned,
if you could only utter forth
odd words made fast with tears and sighs.

You saw the force that struck our heart
– her air, her grace, her dignity.
Now, my little spirits, find
a language that may comfort him.

I see her image rise before us
– beauteous form from high above –
each time the shock dispels our strength.

And then, my little sprites, find speech
to soothe our troubled soul, tell her
she always will belong to Love.

8

L'anima mia vilment' è sbigotita
de la battaglia ch'e[l]l'ave dal core:
che s'ella sente pur un poco Amore
più presso a lui che non sòle, ella more.

Sta come quella che non ha valore,   5
ch'è per temenza da lo cor partita;
e chi vedesse com' ell'è fuggita
diria per certo: "Questi non ha vita".

Per li occhi venne la battaglia in pria,
che ruppe ogni valore immantenente,   10
sì che del colpo fu strutta la mente.

Qualunqu'è quei che più allegrezza sente,
se vedesse li spiriti fuggir via,
di grande sua pietate piangeria.

8

My soul is meanly shaken and knows fear,
and can't resist the siege made on the heart:
if she but feels the mettle of Love's dart
pinch deeper still, Death will prise them apart.

Now overwhelmed by fright she quits the heart,
her vital energy has disappeared:
anyone who saw her flee would swear,
amazed, 'this man lacks life and yet stands here'.

Through the eyes the battle came at first
and quickly broke my vital strength and will,
with such a force my mind was all but killed.

Whoever lives light-hearted in this world
would, if they knew their vital spirits fled
and the mind's pain, cry out, 'I have seen the worst'.

9

Tu m'hai sì piena di dolor la mente,
che l'anima si briga di partire,
e li sospir' che manda 'l cor dolente
mostrano agli occhi che non può soffrire.

Amor, che lo tuo grande valor sente,   5
dice: "E' mi duol che ti convien morire
per questa fiera donna, che nïente
par che pietate di te voglia udire".

I' vo come colui ch'è fuor di vita,
che pare, a chi lo sguarda, ch'omo sia   10
fatto di rame o di pietra o di legno,

che si conduca sol per maestria
e porti ne lo core una ferita
che sia, com' egli è morto, aperto segno.

9

Lady, you fill my mind with suffering.
My soul plots how it might get free,
and the sighs my heart sends forth wring
my eyes: we can't endure such misery.

Love, who knows your worthiness, has said,
'It saddens me that you must die,
but she will let no word of kindness
kindle sign of mercy in her eye'.

I am held in a state of lifelessness
as one who seems to be of human kind,
likened from stuff of copper, wood, or stone,

moved to semblance by man's artifice,
who bears a wound within his heart as sign
that how he died be ever after known.

10

Io non pensava che lo cor giammai
avesse di sospir' tormento tanto,
che dell'anima mia nascesse pianto
mostrando per lo viso agli occhi morte.
    Non sentìo pace né riposo alquanto   5
poscia ch'Amore e madonna trovai,
lo qual mi disse: "Tu non camperai,
ché troppo è lo valor di costei forte".
    La mia virtù si partìo sconsolata
poi che lassò lo core   10
a la battaglia ove madonna è stata:
    la qual degli occhi suoi venne a ferire
in tal guisa, ch'Amore
ruppe tutti miei spiriti a fuggire.

Di questa donna non si può contare: 15
ché di tante bellezze adorna vène,
che mente di qua giù no la sostene
sì che la veggia lo 'ntelletto nostro.
    Tant' è gentil che, quand' eo penso bene,
l'anima sento per lo cor tremare,   20
sì come quella che non pò durare
davanti al gran valor ch'è i llei dimostro.
    Per gli occhi fere la sua claritate,
sì che quale mi vede
dice: "Non guardi tu questa pietate   25
    ch'è posta invece di persona morta
per dimandar merzede?"
E non si n'è madonna ancor accorta!

10

Never would I have thought the heart contained
a host of sighs so troubling that tears
would well up in the soul and show
Death's shadow cast across my cheek.
  Since Love and that dear lady crossed my path
I've had no peace or rest at all.
Love said, 'I do not think you will survive,
her force and will are far too strong.'
  My own strength vanished at these words, and left
the heart alone
to fight in battle with my lady,
she whose eyes had made a wound
so wide that Love
scattered my spirits from their line.

No one can show in words this lady's worth,
for she is so adorned and beautiful
that minds born here on earth can't hold
her image in the intellect.
  And when I dwell on her I feel
how my soul trembles in my heart
like one who must relinquish life,
such is the strength of will she manifests.
  Her splendor struck in through my eyes and now
whoever sees me
cries, 'Behold this pitiful object who
has taken on the guise of Death
to ask for mercy.'
Yet, it seems she is aware of nothing!

Quando 'l pensier mi vèn ch'i' voglia dire
a gentil core de la sua vertute,   30
i' trovo me di sì poca salute,
ch'i' non ardisco di star nel pensero.
    Amor, c'ha le bellezze sue vedute,
mi sbigottisce sì, che sofferire
non può lo cor sentendola venire,   35
ché sospirando dice: "Io ti dispero,
    però che trasse del su' dolce riso
una saetta aguta,
c'ha passato 'l tuo core e 'l mio diviso.
    Tu sai, quando venisti, ch'io ti dissi,   40
poi che l'avéi veduta,
per forza convenia che tu morissi."

Canzon, tu sai che de' libri d'Amore
io t'asemplai quando madonna vidi:
ora ti piaccia ch'io di te mi fidi   45
e vadi 'n guis' a lei, ch'ella t'ascolti;
    e prego umilemente a lei tu guidi
li spiriti fuggiti del mio core,
che per soverchio de lo su' valore
eran distrutti, se non fosser vòlti,   50
    e vanno soli, senza compagnia,
e son pien' di paura.
Però li mena per fidata via
    e poi le di', quando le se' presente:
"Questi sono in figura   55
d'un che si more sbigottitamente".

When the will arises to find words
and tell my lady's worth to noble hearts
I lack the health of mind to hold
the vision of her form before my eye.
  Love who has felt the measure of her beauty
frets me so that even the sight
of her is too much for my heart,
for he reminds me, 'I held little hope
  once she had shot from that sweet smile
the arrow
which has split your heart and pierces mine.
You know that when I met you first I told
how having seen her
meant that you would surely die.'

Canzon, you know that having seen my lady
I then modelled you on the books of Love.
Now must I put my trust in you
to seek her that she hear our song;
  and may you forge a path to lead
my spirits who have fled the heart:
when she appeared they were so overwhelmed
they scattered, fearing for their lives.
  Since then they wander all alone and fear
the slightest sound.
Guide them safely on the way
and when you are before her say
these spirits have
the form of one who dies most fretfully.

11

Poi che di doglia cor conven ch'i' porti
e senta di piacere ardente foco
e di virtù mi traggi' a sì vil loco,
dirò com' ho perduto ogni valore.
    E dico che' miei spiriti son morti,   5
e 'l cor che tanto ha guerra e vita poco;
e se non fosse che 'l morir m'è gioco,
fare'ne di pietà pianger Amore.
    Ma, per lo folle tempo che m'ha giunto,
mi cangio di mia ferma oppinïone   10
in altrui condizione,
sì ch'io non mostro quant' io sento affanno:
là 'nd'eo ricevo inganno,
ché dentro da lo cor mi pass' Amanza,
che se ne porta tutta mia possanza.   15

11

Since mine must be a heart which harbours pain
and feels in place of joy an avid fire,
and since I drag my virtue through the mire,
I'll tell you how I lost my dignity.
    I tell you all my will to live has gone.
My heart has battled hard but starts to tire,
and if death's truce weren't all that I desire
I'd make Love weep in pity seeing me.
    But madness now possesses us,
my constant self is lost in change
to states most strange,
and hence I haven't means to show my pain
which thereby makes more gains;
for Love has struck a path into my heart
and carried off my strength with subtle art.

12

Perché non fuoro a me gli occhi dispenti
o tolti, sì che de la lor veduta
non fosse nella mente mia venuta
a dir: "Ascolta se nel cor mi senti?"

Ch' una paura di novi tormenti   5
m'aparve allor, sì crudel e aguta,
che l'anima chiamò: Donna, or ci aiuta,
che gli occhi ed i' non rimagnàn dolenti!

Tu gli ha' lasciati sì, che venne Amore
a pianger sovra lor pietosamente,   10
tanto che s'ode una profonda voce

la quale dice: "Chi gran pena sente
guardi costui, e vederà 'l su' core
che Morte 'l porta 'n man tagliato in croce"."

12

Why weren't these eyes of mine made blind,
or gouged out, so that through their sight
she'd never forced a way into the mind
to taunt: 'Surely your heart can hear me now!'

Then I was gripped by fear of suffering,
panic increased until my soul cried, 'Lady
help us that the eyes and I
may leave such agony behind.

You have abandoned them to such a fate,
Love weeps in pity seeing how they smart,
and now a voice that heralds from the depths

says, "he who dwells on his own dismal state
observe this man, for one may see his heart
carved like a cross and held in the hand of Death". "

13

Quando di morte mi conven trar vita
e di pesanza gioia,
come di tanta noia
lo spirito d'amor d'amar m'invita?

Come m'invita lo meo cor d'amare,   5
lasso, ch'è pien di doglia
e di sospir' sì d'ogni parte priso,
   che quasi sol merzé non pò chiamare,
e di vertù lo spoglia
l'afanno che m'ha già quasi conquiso?   10
   Canto, piacere, beninanza e riso
me 'n son dogli' e sospiri:
guardi ciascuno e miri
che Morte m'è nel viso già salita!

Amor, che nasce di simil piacere,   15
dentro lo cor si posa
formando di disio nova persona;
   ma fa la sua virtù in vizio cadere,
sì ch'amar già non osa
qual sente come servir guiderdona.   20
   Dunque d'amar perché meco ragiona?
Credo sol perché vede
ch'io domando mercede
a Morte, ch'a ciascun dolor m'adita.

13

If out of death I make my life
and draw all joy from pain,
why does that force remain
which lures me to love?

How can my heart bid me to love
if, overcome by grief,
in every part dispirited,
    he hardly gathers strength enough
to supplicate relief
from pain which causes us this dread?
    Rapture, laughter, song and joy
have turned to woe for me:
he who observes shall see
my countenance casts death, not life.

Love, invoked by similar talent,
reigns within the heart
and forms a figure of desire,
    but makes all virtue fall to vice.
None would honour Love's harsh terms
who knew the guerdon given in reward.
    So why must Love still tempt me with false hope?
Only because he sees
how I beg Death for mercy,
Death, who singles me out for a wretched life.

I' mi posso blasmar di gran pesanza   25
più che nessun giammai:
ché Morte d'entro 'l cor me tragge un core
    che va parlando di crudele amanza,
che ne' mie' forti guai
m'affanna là ond' i' prendo ogni valore.   30
    Quel punto maladetto sia, ch'Amore
nacque di tal manera
cha la mia vita fera
li fue, di tal piacere, a lui gradita.

I more than any other may
lament my present lot,
for Death jeers at my heart, and makes
    a form arise therein that taunts me
speaking of cruel love
and leaving chaos in its wake.
    May all the cruellest curses take
revenge on Love for how
he gloats at
every torment in my life.

14

Io temo che la mia disaventura
non faccia sì ch'i' dica: "I' mi dispero,"
però ch'i' sento nel cor un pensero
che fa tremar la mente di paura,

e par che dica: "Amor non t'assicura   5
in guisa, che tu possi di leggero
a la tua donna sì contar il vero,
che Morte non ti ponga 'n sua figura."

De la gran doglia che l'anima sente
si parte de lo core uno sospiro   10
che va dicendo: "Spiriti, fuggite."

Allor d'un uom che sia pietoso miro,
che consolasse mia vita dolente
dicendo: "Spiritei, non vi partite!"

14

I fear misfortune leads me to that brink
where all I utter is, 'despair.'
Thoughts surface in the heart and cause
the mind to tremble, for they say,

'Love will fail to give you strength
when Death has cast you in her sight,
you'll find yourself before your lady
wanting words that tell your tale of pain.'

Then to aid the troubled soul
the heart sends forth sharp sighs that say,
'My little spirits of life, disband!'

And so I seek for one whose care
can sooth my troubled life and say,
'Oh, little spirits, don't disperse.'

PART 4

In Praise of Love

15

Un amoroso sguardo spiritale
m'ha renovato Amor, tanto piacente
ch'assa' più che non sòl ora m'assale
e stringem' a pensar coralemente

della mia donna, verso cu' non vale   5
merzede né pietà né star soffrente,
ché soventora mi dà pena tale,
che 'n poca parte il mi' cor vita sente.

Ma quando sento che sì dolce sguardo
d'entro degli occhi mi passò lo core   10
e posevi uno spirito di gioia,

di farne a lei mercé, di ciò non tardo:
così pregata foss' ella d'Amore
ch'un poco di pietà no i fosse noia!

15

The spirit of a noble amorous gaze,
guided by Love, has taken hold of me
and fills me with such joy it conquers rage,
drawing me on to think whole-heartedly

of her, my lady, who is not touched by phrase
of tribute, or sign of patience, or piety:
indeed the cruel, relentless games she plays
cause death to grip my heart's vitality.

But when I feel her gaze of radiance
which, through my eyes, passes to the heart
and places there a spirit of delight,

I rush again to offer recompense:
equally, I wish that Love would plead my part
with her, to take some pity on my plight!

16

Veggio negli occhi de la donna mia
un lume pien di spiriti d'amore,
che porta uno piacer novo nel core,
sì che vi desta d'allegrezza vita.

Cosa m'aven, quand' i' le son presente,   5
ch'i' no la posso a lo 'ntelletto dire:
   veder mi par de la sua labbia uscire
una sì bella donna, che la mente
   comprender no la può, che 'mmantenente
ne nasce un'altra di bellezza nova,   10
da la qual par ch'una stella si mova
e dica: "La salute tua è apparita".

Là dove questa bella donna appare
s'ode una voce che le vèn davanti
   e par che d'umilità il su' nome canti   15
sì dolcemente, che, s'i' 'l vo' contare,
   sento che 'l su' valor mi fa tremare;
e movonsi nell'anima sospiri
che dicon: "Guarda; se tu coste' miri,
vedra' la sua vertù nel ciel salita".   20

16

In my lady's eyes I see
a light filled with such spirits of love
it brings my heart new hope of
being once more inspired to life.

In her presence I am overcome
by a sight beyond intelligence,
    for from within her countenance
a woman of beauty is born who numbs
    all cognisance, and there in turn one
newer marvel materialises,
out of which a star soon rises
saying, 'Here is your hope of life'.

And where this beautiful woman appears
a voice is heard which calls her name,
    so gently does it sing her fame
I cannot now recount the sound,
    no words for such will ever be found;
while sighs which shift within the soul
say, 'See her, and behold
her virtue rising to eternal life'.

17

Pegli occhi fere un spirito sottile,
che fa 'n la mente spirito destare,
dal qual si move spirito d'amare,
ch'ogn'altro spiritel fa[ce] gentile.

Sentir non pò di lu' spirito vile,   5
di cotanta vertù spirito appare:
quest'è lo spiritel che fa tremare,
lo spiritel che fa la donna umìle.

E poi da questo spirito si move
un altro dolce spirito soave,   10
che siegue un spiritello di mercede:

lo quale spiritel spiriti piove,
ché di ciascuno spirit' ha la chiave,
per forza d'uno spirito che 'l vede.

17

At first a spirit enters through the eyes
and stirs a spirit in the mind
from whence a sprite of Love draws life
that lifts each vital spirit up in joy.

Just-spirited and noble hearts alone
may know Love's spirit full of worth,
a spirit that will baffle men,
a spirit stronger that the proudest lady.

This same sprite gives life in turn
to a spirit full of calm and grace,
and then at last to Mercy's little spirit

who seeds a shower of spirited sighs,
for he holds each vital spirit's key,
now he is manifest to the spirit of sight.

PART 5

Love Defined

18

Donna me prega, per ch'eo voglio dire
d'un accidente che sovente è fero
ed è sì altero ch'è chiamato amore:
    sì chi lo nega possa 'l ver sentire!
Ed a presente conoscente chero,   5
perch'io no spero ch'om di basso core
    a tal ragione porti canoscenza:
ché senza natural dimostramento
non ho talento di voler provare
là dove posa, e chi lo fa creare,   10
    e qual sia sua vertute e sua potenza,
l'essenza poi e ciascun suo movimento,
e 'l piacimento che 'l fa dire amare,
e s'omo per veder lo pò mostrare.

In quella parte dove sta memora   15
prende suo stato, sì formato, come
diaffan da lume, d'una scuritate
    la qual da Marte vène, e fa demora;
elli è creato (ed ha, sensato, nome),
d'alma costume e di cor volontate.   20
    Vèn da veduta forma che s'intende,
che prende nel possibile intelletto,
come in subietto, loco e dimoranza.
In quella parte mai non ha possanza
    perché da qualitate non descende: 25
resplende in sé perpetüal effetto;
non ha diletto ma consideranza;
sì che non pote largir simiglianza.

18

Because a lady bids me I would speak
of an insubstantial thing that is so fierce
and powerful it bears the name of Love.
    And let those who deny it feel the truth!
To speak at all I'll need a learned audience,
for there's no hope that an ignoble heart
    will understand such reasoning as this,
built as it is from natural proofs
and without which I'd lack the skill to show
where Love will dwell, what forces give it birth,
    the nature of its strengths and qualities,
its essence, next, and what it stirs in man,
the joy by which it takes the name of Love,
and, finally, if it be visible.

Within that zone of man where memory lies
Love is given shape by a darkness born of Mars
(just as one finds transparency is given
    form by light), and quickly makes its home:
it takes a sensate name, will from the heart,
and costume from the soul, and thus it claims its being.
    It enters when an object caught by sight
takes up in the potential intellect,
as in a substance, form and residence.
But there Love has no strength of will, since one's
    potential intellect does not derive from qualities;
rather, it shines its own light on eternal things,
dwelling not on pleasure, but contemplation,
and thus creates no point of paragon.

Non è vertute, ma da quella vène
ch'è perfezione (ché si pone tale),   30
non razionale, ma che sente, dico;
    for di salute giudicar mantene,
ché la 'ntenzione per ragione vale:
discerne male in cui è vizio amico.
      Di sua potenza segue spesso morte,   35
se forte la vertù fosse impedita
la quale aita la contraria via:
non perché oppost' a naturale sia;
    ma quanto che da buon perfetto tort' è
per sorte, non pò dire om ch'aggia vita,   40
ché stabilita non ha segnoria.
A simil pò valer quand'om l'oblia.

L'essere è quando lo voler è tanto
ch'oltra misura di natura torna,
poi non s'adorna di riposo mai.   45
    Move, cangiando color, riso in pianto,
e la figura con paura storna;
poco soggiorna; ancor di lui vedrai
    che 'n gente di valor lo più si trova.
La nova qualità move sospiri,   50
e vol ch'om miri 'n non formato loco,
destandos' ira la qual manda foco
    (imaginar nol pote om che nol prova),
né mova già però ch'a lui si tiri,
e non si giri, per trovarvi gioco,   55
né certamente gran saver né poco.

Though not itself a faculty, Love comes
from one: perfection not of the rational
but of the sensitive nature of man; and so
    beyond the bounds of sanity Love casts
our judgement, letting impulse weigh on measured thought:
a man controlled by passion lacks discernment.
    Love's potency will often lead to death
because it can obstruct the vital spirits
working towards the opposite effect;
not that Love is opposed to human nature,
    but who diverges from the perfect good
can hardly claim he lives life well,
he lacks authority to rule himself,
like those who may forget that good.

The pith of Love is a desire so strong
it breaks with nature's limits. From then on
there is no harmony in life.
    Leaving the lover's face transformed by fear,
or causing change to hue and mood, it alters
as it comes and goes, a restlessness
    that seeks out those of worth above all others.
Craving novelty, it fosters sighs,
and forces one to fix on unformed things,
awakening anger which then stirs up fire
    (experience alone can tell you this);
it won't permit one turn one's gaze
to look elsewhere in search of help,
or light relief, or wisdom great or small.

De simil tragge complessione sguardo
che fa parere lo piacere certo:
non pò coverto star, quand'è sì giunto.

   Non già selvagge le bieltà son dardo,   60
ché tal volere per temere è sperto:
consiegue merto spirito ch'è punto.

   E non si pò conoscer per lo viso:
compriso, bianco in tale obietto cade;
e, chi ben aude, forma non si vede: 65
dunqu' elli meno, che da lei procede.

   For di colore, d'essere diviso,
assiso 'n mezzo scuro, luce rade.
For d'ogne fraude dico, degno in fede,
che solo di costui nasce mercede.   70

Tu puoi sicuramente gir, canzone,
là 've ti piace, ch'io t'ho sì adornata
ch'assai laudata sarà tua ragione
da le persone c'hanno intendimento:
di star con l'altre tu non hai talento.   75

Love links us with a glance to someone similar,
so pleasure seems a certainty,
and at this point it cannot stay concealed.
   What's beautiful, unless ignoble, is his arrow,
since baser fear disperses Love's desire,
so one, when struck, receives his just deserts.
   Not visible per se, Love, comprehended,
is a whiteness in the sensitive soul,
for as one knows form cannot be perceived,
much less, then, Love which does but come from form.
   Devoid of colour, lacking its own being,
found in darkness, ending light,
Love alone, I say, must clearly be
our single fruitful source of mercy.

My song, securely may you roam with pride,
where ever you wish, for you are so adorned
with beauty that your reasoning shall be praised
by those who have a knowledge of such things,
while you may well ignore all other ears.

PART 6

Other Loves

19

Una giovane donna di Tolosa,
bell' e gentil, d'onesta leggiadria,
è tant' e dritta e simigliante cosa,
ne' suoi dolci occhi, della donna mia,

che fatt' ha dentro al cor disiderosa   5
l'anima, in guisa che da lui si svia
e vanne a lei; ma tant' è paurosa,
che no le dice di qual donna sia.

Quella la mira nel su' dolce sguardo,
ne lo qual face rallegrare Amore   10
perché v'è dentro la sua donna dritta;

po' torna, piena di sospir', nel core,
ferita a morte d'un tagliente dardo
che questa donna nel partir li gitta.

19

A noble young Toulousian lady,
graceful and of honourable guise,
so closely mirrors my own lady,
especially in her charming eyes,

that she has stirred the soul which lay
within the heart, until he rises,
drawn to her, but slow to say,
for fear, with whom he usually lies.

The soul admires her gaze of light
where Love is woken to delight
for their own lady seems a twin;

but then he draws back to the heart
mortally wounded by a dart
which she, on leaving, shot at him.

20

Era in penser d'amor quand'i' trovai
due foresette nove.
L'una cantava: "E' piove
gioco d'amore in noi".

Era la vista lor tanto soave   5
e tanto queta, cortese e umìle,
    ch'i' dissi lor: "Vo' portate la chiave
di ciascuna vertù alta e gentile.
    Deh, foresette, no m'abbiate a vile
per lo colpo ch'io porto;   10
questo cor mi fue morto
poi che 'n Tolosa fui".

Elle con gli occhi lor si volser tanto
che vider come 'l cor era ferito
    e come un spiritel nato di pianto   15
era per mezzo de lo colpo uscito.
    Poi che mi vider così sbigottito,
disse l'una, che rise:
"Guarda come conquise
forza d'amor costui"!   20

L'altra, pietosa, piena di mercede,
fatta di gioco in figura d'Amore,
    disse: "'L tuo colpo, che nel cor si vede,
fu tratto d'occhi di troppo valore,
    che dentro vi lasciaro uno splendore   25
ch'i' nol posso mirare.
Dimmi se ricordare
di quegli occhi ti puoi".

20

Deep in thoughts of love I met
by chance two country girls.
One sang, 'the rains of Love
fall softly in our hearts'.

So pleasing was the sight of them,
their air so quiet and courteous,
    that I was moved to speak, 'Dear girls,
you carry every virtue's key.
    Please do not hold me in disdain
despite my wounded heart:
he met with Death
when I was in Toulouse'.

They turned with curiosity
and saw the way my heart was struck
    and where a spirit born of tears
came sighing from the wound.
    Seeing me so weak and shaken
one then smiled and said,
'Look how Love's strength
has conquered this proud man'.

The second, like a figure of Love
forged from joy and empathy,
    spoke next, 'The wound within your heart
was caused by eyes of highest worth;
    a radiance now rests in you
I dare not look upon.
But if you may, please
tell us of those eyes'.

Alla dura questione e paurosa
la qual mi fece questa foresetta,   30
    i' dissi: "E' mi ricorda che 'n Tolosa
donna m'apparve accordellata istretta,
    Amor la qual chaimava la Mandetta;
giunse sì presta e forte,
che fin dentro, a la morte,   35
mi colpîr gli occhi suoi".

Molto cortesemente mi rispuose
quella che di me prima avëa riso.
    Disse: "La donna che nel cor ti pose
co la forza d'amor tutto 'l su' viso,   40
    dentro per li occhi ti mirò sì fiso,
ch'Amor fece apparire.
Se t'è greve 'l soffrire,
raccomàndati a lui".

Vanne a Tolosa, ballatetta mia,   45
ed entra quetamente a la Dorata,
    ed ivi chiama che per cortesia
d'alcuna bella donna sie menata
    dinanzi a quella di cui t'ho pregata;
e s'ella ti riceve,   50
dille con voce leve:
"Per merzé vegno a voi".

Her question left me trembling;
eventually I conquered fear
    and said, 'While I was in Toulouse
a lady dressed most nobly,
    whom Love addressed by name, Mandetta,
struck my eye
so forcefully she left
me on the brink of death.'

The first girl who had smiled at me
now spoke again most cordially,
    'The lady reigning in your heart
held in her gaze the force of Love
    and looked so deeply in your eyes
that Love appeared in you.
If suffering is hard
then turn to him for help.'

Go, my ballatteta, to Toulouse
and enter gently by the door
    of the Dorata. Cordially ask
if any lady there will lead you
    to the woman we have loved.
And if she does receive you
tell her with soft voice
'I come to ask for mercy.'

21

In un boschetto trova' pasturella
più che la stella bella, al mi' parere.

Cavelli avea biondetti e ricciutelli,
e gli occhi pien' d'amor, cera rosata;
   con sua verghetta pasturav' agnelli;   5
[di]scalza, di rugiaga era bagnata;
   cantava come fosse 'namorata:
er' adornata di tutto piacere.

D'amor la saluta' imantenente
e domandai s'avesse compagnia;   10
   ed ella mi rispose dolzemente
che sola sola per lo bosco gia,
   e disse: "Sacci, quando l'augel pia,
allor disïa 'l me' cor drudo avere".

Po' che mi disse di sua condizione   15
e per lo bosco augelli audìo cantare,
   fra me stesso diss' i': "Or è stagione
di questa pasturella gio' pigliare".
   Merzé le chiesi sol che di basciare
ed abracciar, se le fosse 'n volere.   20

Per man mi prese, d'amorosa voglia,
e disse che donato m'avea 'l core;
   menòmmi sott'una freschetta foglia,
là dov' i' vidi fior' d'ogni colore;
   e tanto vi sentìo gioia e dolzore,   25
che 'l die d'amore mi parea vedere.

21

Within a wood I met a shepherd girl
who seemed more lovely than the stars to me.

Her hair fell down in locks of gold,
her feet were bare and wet with dew,
    she watched her lambs with eyes made bold
by youth that thirsts for life's bright hue;
    she sang of Love as one who knew
his realm and how he worships beauty.

With amorous words I greeted her
and asked if she had friends nearby;
    to which with such sweet voice she said
she ranged alone the cool woodside,
    and then, 'whenever songbirds cry
my heart begins to long for company.'

She spoke so freely of her state
and all the birds were chorusing;
    I told myself, do not wait,
but share with her some pleasuring;
    I asked if she would like to pause
awhile to talk and love sweet life with me.

Amorously she took my hand
and said that now her heart was mine;
    she led me where spring's flowers span
the fields in a thousand colours and kinds,
    and there I knew a joy so fine
I felt the God of love sigh deep in me.

PART 7

Exile and Epilogue

22

Perch'i' no spero di tornar giammai,
ballatetta, in Toscana,
va' tu, leggera e piana,
dritt' a la donna mia,
che per la sua cortesia   5
ti farà molto onore.

Tu porterai novelle di sospiri
piene di dogl' e di molta paura;
    ma guarda che persona non ti miri
che sia nemica di gentil natura: 10
    ché certo per la mia disaventura
tu saresti contesa,
tanto da lei ripresa
che mi sarebbe angoscia;
dopo la morte, poscia,   15
pianto e novel dolore.

Tu senti, ballatetta, che la morte
mi stringe sì, che vita m'abbandona;
    e senti come 'l cor si sbatte forte
per quel che ciascun spirito ragiona.   20
    Tanto è distrutta già la mia persona,
ch'i' non posso soffrire:
se tu mi vuoi servire,
mena l'anima teco
(molto di ciò ti preco)   25
quando uscirà del core.

22

Because I do not hope to turn again
to Tuscany,
my ballatetta, go for me
straight to my lady, who,
for all her graciousness
is sure to welcome you.

You shall take word of me composed in sighs
which tell of suffering and countless fears;
    but please be careful to avoid the eyes
of those who do not hold nobility dear:
    insensible to my misfortune here
they would misconstrue
and falsely censure you,
then no hope would be sound
as even in death I found
my present pain renewed.

You, ballatetta, understand how tight
Death's present hold is on my life,
    and feel how my heart beats out of control
because each vital spirit speaks of strife.
    Our body is abased because pain stifles
any higher thoughts.
If you would lend support
then take along my soul
which clearly bears the toll
of Love, I beg you.

Deh, ballatetta, a la tu' amistate
quest'anima che trema raccomando:
   menala teco, nella sua pietate,
a quella bella donna a cu' ti mando.   30
   Deh, ballatetta, dille sospirando,
quando le se' presente:
"Questa vostra servente
vien per istar con voi,
partita da colui   35
che fu servo d'Amore".

Tu, voce sbigottita e deboletta
ch'esci piangendo de lo cor dolente,
   coll'anima e con questa ballatetta
va' ragionando della strutta mente.   40
   Voi troverete una donna piacente,
di sì dolce intelletto
che vi sarà diletto
starle davanti ognora.
Anim', e tu l'adora   45
sempre, nel su' valore.

To you I recommend this trembling soul,
my ballatetta, and to our amity.
     Carry her with you - for she bears Love's toll -
where you are sent before nobility.
     And ballatetta, once before my lady
speak of us in sighs,
'Here behold, your highness,
a soul, which leaving one
who served Love well, now comes
to serve and be with you.'

You, my voice, revealing how you fret
where you stutter forth through tears from the heart,
     with the soul and with this ballatetta
go and speak of how my mind now smarts.
     The lady you encounter through your art
evokes joy beyond measure,
and nurtures noblest pleasure.
May you stay before her,
and with the soul adore her -
her valour shall always be true.

23

Noi siàn le triste penne isbigotite,
le cesoiuzze e 'l coltellin dolente,
ch'avemo scritte dolorosamente
quelle parole che vo' avete udite.

Or vi diciàn perché noi siàn partite   5
e siàn venute a voi qui di presente:
la man che ci movea dice che sente
cose dubbiose nel core apparite;

le quali hanno destrutto sì costui
ed hannol posto sì presso a la morte,   10
ch'altro non n'è rimaso che sospiri.

Or vi preghiàn quanto possiàn più forte
che non sdegniate di tenerci noi,
tanto ch'un poco di pietà vi miri.

23

We are the stunned and mourning quill,
the doleful knife and tiny shears
who painfully, with all our skill,
contrived those words which found your ears.

Now let us tell you why we travelled
and hope to sway you through our art:
our guiding hand says she is held
by strange apparitions in the heart.

How these have often troubled us
and forced the heart to sigh for death
exceeds our talent to narrate.

With all our strength we pray you will
hold back disdain to hear our voice
and take some pity on our state.

ANNOTATIONS

AUTHOR'S NOTE

Where reference is made to a comment by another editor bibliographic information is not provided unless it is unclear where the comment comes from. Otherwise it is presumed that the comment may be found in the notes to the poem in question in the relevant edition. Likewise where reference is made to other English translations the same principle applies. In general the versions by Pound and Rossetti are used as points of comparison. A fuller discussion of these two translators can be found in the introduction. The edition by Lowry Nelson published in 1986 is also referred to regularly. Other occasional translations are called on where they exist, as indicated in the introduction to each poem. Quotations from Dante's lyric poetry are followed by the English version in *Dante's Lyric Poetry,* edited and translated by Kenelm Foster and Patrick Boyde, Oxford 1967. Translations of passages from the *Vita Nuova* are taken from Mark Musa, *Dante's Vita Nuova*, Indiana University Press, 1973. Quotations from the *Commedia* are followed by the Allen Mandelbaum translation in the Everyman Library, 1995. Quotations from Guinizzelli make use of the English version, *The Poetry of Guido Guinizzelli*, edited and translated by Robert Edwards, Garland Publishing 1987.

Poems by Cavalcanti are referred to using the numbering in the present edition. Where reference is made to a poem not found in this selection the full first line is given. Unless otherwise stated the text of Cavalcanti's poetry follows the edition by Domenico De Robertis.

PART ONE: EARLY POEMS

1 – *Biltà di donna e di saccente core*
2 – *Chi è questa che vèn, ch'ogn'om la mira*

The two sonnets translated here, along with the ballad 'Fresca rosa novella' and the sonnet 'Avete 'n vo' li fior'e la verdura' (neither of which are included in the present selection), are almost certainly early works. They reveal the strong influence both of the Sicilian School, and of Guinizzelli. There are archaising elements in the prosody and language not found in Cavalcanti's other poetry. These two poems are more easily identifiable as belonging to set genres, respectively a *plazer* and a praise poem. But already there are signs of the originality, vigour of language and attention to craftsmanship which were to make Cavalcanti such a startling and influential poet.

1 *BILTÀ DI DONNA E DI SACCENTE CORE*

This sonnet belongs to the genre known as the *plazer* (Provençal word for 'pleasure'), a composition frequent in Provençal poetry in which the loved object (invariably a lady) is praised for her spiritual and physical beauty through a series of comparisons. The genre took the form of a list of things that give pleasure and offer beauty, all of which are shown to fall short of the lady in question. Often the points of comparison were taken from a limited stock pertaining to the natural world and to courtly life.[1] Giacomo da Lentini's 'Diamante, né smiraldo, né zaffiro' is an early Italian example. But it was very popular elsewhere too, and its influence can still be seen in Shakespeare's sonnets 'Shall I compare thee to a summer's day' and 'My mistress' eyes are nothing like the sun', which gain much of their power from the subversion of the expectations of the genre.

In 'Biltà di donna' the comparisons are divided into two groups: to courtly life (lines 1-4), and to nature (lines 5-8). The comparisons themselves are fairly conventional. Yet the delicate manner in which they are arranged is unique. This creates something of a dreamy atmosphere, or, as Italo Calvino described it in *Lezioni americane*, a sense of lightness: 'tutto si muove così rapidamente che non possiamo renderci conto della sua consistenza ma solo dei suoi effetti' [everything moves so quickly that we cannot grasp the consistency but only the effects] (Calvino 17). Furthermore this particular sonnet has had an important influence on the subsequent tradition: Dante is wrestling with the beautiful control of line 6 in *Inferno* XIV, 30; and Petrarch clearly wrote sonnet CCCXII of the *Canzoniere* in homage to Cavalcanti's composition.

'Biltà di donna' takes as a model Guinizzelli's praise sonnet, 'Io voglio del ver la mia donna laudare', line 7 of which, 'oro ed azzurro e ricche gioi per dare', is echoed here in line 8, 'oro, argento, azzuro 'n ornamenti'. Like Guinizzelli, Cavalcanti combines the listing structure of the *plazer* in the octet with a more generic praise poem in the sestet, in which the lady now surpasses all forms of comparison. This is an idea developed in the next poem, where such religious overtones become clearer.

For the translator, the difficulty is to reproduce the placidity and lightness of the atmosphere, without the conventional descriptions sounding trite. There are versions by Rossetti (III. Sonnet: He compares all Things with his Lady, and finds them wanting) and Pound (1912). Fraser and Goldin also produced versions of this poem. Goldin translates in a fluid prose,while Fraser uses iambic pentameter and maintains Cavalcanti's rhyme scheme.

STRUCTURAL NOTE

The rhyme scheme is ABAB ABAB CDE CDE. In the quatrains ABAB, is the so-called 'archaic' scheme found most commonly in early Italian poetry. From the *stilnovo* onwards it was increasingly replaced by ABBA, which is the most common scheme used by Cavalcanti. This is a further indication, though by no means a concrete proof, of an early date of composition.[2] ABBA gives each quatrain a structural balance and

77

autonomy which the continual alteration of A with B in consecutive lines does not allow for. De Robertis notes that the rhymes in –*enti* and –*ore* are also found together in Dante's sonnet 'Sonar bracchetti', a poem with many stylistic similarities.

ANNOTATIONS

Line 1: a literal translation of this first line might run, 'Beauty of woman and heart of a wise person'. Nelson has 'Woman's beauty and sage's heart'; Rossetti, 'Beauty in woman; the high will's decree'; and Pound, 'Beauty of woman, of the knowing heart'.

biltà: an example of the archaic diction adopted in this sonnet, for *bellezza*, beauty.

di saccente core: 'heart of a wise person'. Thus, inner virtue parallels the external beauty.

Line 2: genti: *gentili*, and therefore 'noble'. The vestige of such a usage of 'gentle' in English is still to be found in 'gentleman'. In *Richard III* the following lines suggest it still had a similar meaning in Shakespeare's time: 'Since every Jack became a gentleman, / There's many a gentle person made a Jack'. (I, iii, 71-72). The nobility in question is that of the spirit, not simply of parentage, for a fuller discussion of which see the canzone by Dante, 'Le dolci rime d'amor ch'i' solia'. Pound has 'And courtly knights in bright accoutrement'. Rossetti has 'Fair knighthood arm'd for manly exercise'.

Line 3: cantar... ragionar...: both of these infinitives are used as nouns. The unification of reason and love is an ideal that Dante was to emphasise in his lyric poetry. See, for example, 'Amor che ne la mente mi ragiona'. It does not find many other expressions in Cavalcanti. What is interesting here is the implicit link between song and reasoning, which recalls Dante's definition of poetry, 'que nichil aliud est quam fictio rethorica musicaque poita' [poetry being nothing other than a creation poetically expressed according to rhetoric and music] (*De Vulgari Eloquentia*, II, iv, 2). English translators have struggled with **ragionar d'amore**, perhaps because the literal 'to reason of love' or 'the reasonings of love' are both clumsy expressions. Pound has 'and loving speeches, and the small bird's art'; Rossetti, 'The pleasant song of birds; love's soft replies'; and Nelson, 'Singing of birds and discoursing of love'.

Line 4: forte: an adverb modifying **correnti**, 'fast'.

adorni legni: 'ornate ships'. **Legno** for ship is quite common in this period.

Line 5: aria: metonymy for 'sky'.

albore: another Provençalism for 'dawn'.

Line 6: e bianca neve scender senza venti: Dante echoes this line in *Inferno* XIV, 30, 'come di neve in alpe sanza vento' [as snow in the mountains without wind].

Line 7: rivera: 'river' rather than 'river-bank', from the French *rivière*. This produces the rather banal literal translation 'river of water' (perhaps with the connotation of 'abundance of water'), and again reveals a poetry written with as much consideration for the rhythms and quality of vowel sounds as for literal meaning. Rossetti's solution was to use a circumlocution, 'the place where waters rise'. Pound has 'Brook-marge and mead where every flower flareth'.

Line 8: azzuro: 'lapis lazuli'.

in ornamento: a rather ambiguous expression, possibly meaning 'in jewelry' or 'in relief'. The three precious metals of the original have been reduced to two in my translation for the benefit of the metre, just as they were probably three in number in the original for the benefit of the hendecasyllable. It should be remembered that in a listing process like this a contemporary reader would have had a sense of greatness in abundance. Similarly two adjectives that are for all intents synonyms will often be found together in *Duecento* poetry, because it was felt that intensity was strengthened by repetition.[3]

Line 9: ciò: a single word encompasses everything contained in the quatrains.

beltate e la valenza: adjectives in symmetry with those in line 1.

valenza: a difficult term to translate. It is frequent in the poetry of both

Cavalcanti and Dante, often in the form *valente*. Taken from Provençal, it has no single English equivalent, but can be said to signify 'the complex of good qualities associated with 'courtly' love' (Foster and Boyde 26). The majority of English translators use 'worth', though Pound uses 'valour'. One finds a similar coupling of worth with beauty in Guinizzelli, 'Vedut'ò la lucente stella diana', line 8, 'sì piena di biltate e di valore'. Cassata, in his version of the poem, follows a second manuscript and prints *piagenza* in place of **valenza**, but given the lack of conclusive arguments for Cassata's choice I have preferred **valenza**.

Line 10: **gentil coraggio**: 'gentile core', or 'noble heart'. Cavalcanti echoes lines 1 and 2, where both these words had cognates at the end of a line. **Coraggio** is an archaic form for *core*. Pound has 'And valour of my Lady's lordly daring'.

Line 11: **rasembra**: 'seems in comparison'. A literal translation might run: 'such that (all that was described in the quatrains) seems in comparison, to whoever sees her, petty'. Rossetti interprets lines 9-11 quite differently: 'Weighed against these the sweet and quiet worth / Which my dear lady cherishes at heart / Might seem a little matter to be shown'.

Line 13: I have favoured Cassata's version over that of De Robertis here. De Robertis reads '*quanto lo ciel de la terra è maggio*', with a diaeresis between *a* and *è*. The strongest paragon is left until last, creating a crescendo effect through the comparisons.

maggio: 'maggiore', greater.

Line 14: **a simil di natura**: 'to a similar creature goodness does not tarry to reach', that is to say, there is no quality lacking in a creature like her (De Robertis). Once again, a more ambivalent line sends the translators off in various directions: Pound has 'Good seeketh out its like with some address'; Fraser, 'To such a one good luck will never tarry'; and Nelson, 'Properly one dwells on such a thing of nature'. Rossetti is, to my ear, the most successful: 'All good to kindred natures cleaveth soon'.

2 *CHI È QUESTA CHE VÈN, CH'OGN'OM LA MIRA*

The early praise style of Cavalcanti is generally considered to culminate in one of his better known poems, 'Chi è questa che vèn'. The influence of Guinizzelli is strong. Poem 2 can be read in relation to the older poet's composition, 'Io voglio del ver', discussed in relation to the previous poem. Here, four rhyme words *âre, pare, vertute, salute* are taken from Guinizzelli's poem. The debt is wittily incorporated into Cavalcanti's sonnet.

Guinizzelli praised his lady by comparing her to the best in nature. As a means of upping the stakes and putting her above nature altogether he then declared that there was something miraculous about her, since she even inspired faith in God. In 'Chi è questa che vèn' the search to find similitudes has been abandoned. The narrator's lady is beyond language, and beyond human comprehension. This theme has a long tradition. It is already present, for example, in Arnaut Daniel where one finds 'A lieis, cui son, vai, chanssos, derenan, / c'Arnautz non sap comtar sas grans ricors, / que d'aussor sen li auria ops espandres'. [To her, to whom I belong, go now my song: / Arnaut doesn't know how to describe her wealth, / it would require a greater genius.] XIII, 43-45; and 'c'una de pretz ab lieis no is pot egar' [since no other woman comes close to being her equal] XV, 30.[4] Cavalcanti, however, not without a hint of irreverence, frames his description in a language which is rich with biblical echoes. The opening line recalls *Isaiah* (63,1), 'Quis est ista qui venit?', with reference to the Messiah. The implication seems to be that the narrator's lady doesn't inspire belief in God, but is a sort of divinity herself. Again, it is the Provençal poet, Arnaut Daniel, in 'En cest sonet coind'e leri', who seems to offer an earlier model for the sacrilegious lover: 'No vuoill de Roma l'emperi / ni c'om m'en fassa apostoli, / qu'en lieis non aia revert / per cui m'art lo cors e'm rima. / E si'l malraich no'm restaura / ab un baiser anz d'annou, / mi auci e si enferna' [I wouldn't want the Roman empire / or even to become an Apostle / if it meant I had to give up her [my lady] / who makes my heart burn until it cracks. / And if she doesn't repair the damage done / with a kiss within the year / she will have killed me and sent herself to hell.] 29-35. In 'Chi è questa che vèn' it is interesting to note how the descriptions of the lady's ineffability take the form of a series of negatives that emphasise, in turn, a negative or imperfect conception of man (De Robertis; Marti 1973, 220).

One can trace a progression through Cavalcanti's four early poems of praise, from an initial association of the lady with love in 'Fresca rosa novella' and 'Avete in voi', to descriptions of the lady's unmatchable perfection in 'Biltà di donna', which is, in turn, replaced in the present sonnet with the proclamation of her ineffable nature (De Robertis, Contini). While this has been done, and can serve to aid our understanding of Cavalcanti, the reader must keep in mind that there are not sufficient elements for an objective ordering of the corpus of poems, and therefore any attempt to trace a progression of artistic development through the poetry remains subjective.

Poem 2 is one of those by Cavalcanti most frequently translated into English. There are versions by Rossetti (IV. Sonnet: A Rapture concerning his Lady), and Pound (three distinct versions, dated 1910, 1912 and 1932). There are also versions by Wilhelm, Fraser, Goldin and Kay. Fraser offers a sonnet in iambic pentameter which maintains the original rhyme scheme, unfortunately to the detriment of lexicon and syntax: line 4, for example, reads '*Alas! How seems she when her eyes she turns*'. Wilhelm has also produced a sonnet which maintains the formal constraints of the original, though his choice of rhyme words shows little care at times: 'Love tells me: 'No, you'd only bumble, / Because of women she's so far most humble'. Both Goldin and Kay provide prose versions.

STRUCTURAL NOTE
The rhyme scheme found here, ABBA ABBA CDE EDC, is that used most frequently by Cavalcanti, in ten of his thirty-six sonnets. The tercets are dominated by *a minore* lines. The first quatrain alternates *a maiore* and *a minore* lines, thus linking lines across the rhyme scheme.

ANNOTATIONS
Lines 1-4: In three of the lines in the first quatrain the caesura is

pronounced, giving the impression of a series of short proclamations or exclamations.

Line 1: Contini traces the biblical allusions to various locations in the *Song of Songs*, as well as *Isaiah* (Contini).

mira: 'gaze upon, fix with one's eye'.

Line 2: tremar di chiaritate l'âre: chiaritate is a latinism for 'light'. Dante picks up this idea in *Inf.* I, 48: 'sì che parea l'aere ne tremesse' [such that it seemed the air trembled as a result]. Literally it would read: 'who makes shimmer with light the air'. The original image refers to the scientific belief of the time which held that the air itself could tremble as a result of the intensity of the light which it carried, whereas we would consider the light to tremble or shimmer due to the movement of air which contains some moisture. Similarly in *Purgatorio* I, 117 'conobbi il tremolar de la marina'; and *Paradiso* II 110-111: '… luce sì vivace / che ti tremolerà nel suo aspetto' (De Robertis). Rossetti is good at this point: 'Who makes the air all tremulous with light'. Pound has 'And makyng the air to tremble with a bright clearenesse' (1932).

Line 3: mena seco: 'leads'.

sì che: 'in such a manner that'.

Lines 3-4: parlar / null'omo pote: 'no one can speak'. In Dante's sonnet 'Tanto gentile, tanto onesta pare' we find 'ch'ogne lingua deven tremando muta' [that all tongues tremble and fall silent].

Line 5: quando li occhi gira: 'whenever her eyes move, or take something in'. Rossetti's 'Ah me! How she looks round from left to right', leaves the reader wondering what all the fuss is about. Pound has 'Ah God! The thing she's like when her glance strays (1912); and 'Ah God, what she is like when her owne eye turneth' (1932).

Line 6: dical Amor: '(I would that) Love told of it'.

nol savria contare: 'I wouldn't know how to describe it'.

Line 7: cotanto d'umiltà: 'so humble or benign'. **Umiltà** is a difficult term to translate. Branca's description is helpful, and demonstrates just how broad the concept was: 'significa insieme mitezza, benignità, serenità, pudore, soavità' (Branca).

Line 8: ch'ogn'altra: parallels line 1 (De Robertis).

ver di lei: 'compared to her'.

i' la chiam'ira: 'I scorn or disdain'. It is difficult to determine the intensity of the noun, *ira*, as the various translations testify. Nelson at this point translates, 'that any other, in comparison to her, I call vexation', which is worth comparing with Pound: 'Such is her modesty, I would call / Every woman else but an useless uneasiness' (1932); and Goldin, 'I call every other woman fury, compared to her'. At the other end of the scale Rossetti has 'As makes all others graceless in men's sight'. The term is best thought of as the opposite of **Umiltà** in line 7, and is found with a similar usage in Dante, 'Ne li occhi porta', line 7, 'fugge dinanzi a lei superbia ed ira' (De Robertis).

Lines 5-8: as a whole the second quatrain contains some interesting linguistic reminders of Arnaut Daniel's poem, 'Can chai la fueilla', which in lines 27-32 runs: 'c'autrui paria / torn ieu en reirazar; / ges ab sa par / no sai doblar m'amia, / c'una non par / que segonda no ill sia'. [since to compare [her] to other women / is to make a bad throw of the dice; / to her equal / I wouldn't be able to compare my friend / for there is no one / who would not come second to her]. The image of gambling evoked by the verb 'reirazar' is similar to that of counting in 'Chi è questa'. Significantly both passages share the same context of the impossibility of comparing the lady to others. The Provençal rhyme, *'par'*, occurs here as *'pare'*, while the other rhyme, –*ira*, is not far from Daniel's –*ia*.

Line 9: contare: also found in line 6.

piagenza: 'pleasure giving'. This is pleasure of a moral or spiritual value as much as of any other kind. The English 'pleasantness' is burdened with connotations of something favourable but far from ecstatic. Pound hoped to avoid this by adopting a pseudo-archaic spelling, 'pleasauntness' (1932). I have followed Nelson and Goldin in changing the attribute to that of grace. Rossetti does the same, though he uses the attribute 'honour'. This seems justified by the qualifications made to **piagenza** in lines 10 and 11 in the original. Wilhelm has 'No one could count her many charms, though modest'; Fraser, 'Uncounted are the gifts which make her rich'.

Line 10: s'inchina: either 'bows down before' or 'inclines towards'.

Line 11: sua dea: possibly a hint of Cavalcanti's irreverence, though De Robertis suggests *dea* is closer to 'ideal' or 'perfection' here than Goddess, and traces it back to Guittone.

Line 12: la mente nostra: 'our (human) knowledge or understanding'. The lady is positioned in opposition not only to the narrator but to all of humanity.

Line 13: salute: perfection. Pound has 'Nor have we so much of heal as will afford' (1932).

Line 14: propiamente: fully.

aviàn: *abbiamo*.

n'aviàn canoscenza: 'have an understanding or knowledge of her'. Rossetti has 'That we should ever know her perfectly'; by contrast, the later Pound seems clumsy, 'That our thought may take her immediate in its embrace' (1932). In 1912 Pound had 'That we can understand her rightfully'. Wilhelm has 'To encompass her and say, "I understand"'.

PART TWO: SONNETS ADDRESSED TO DANTE

3 – *Vedeste, al mio parere, onne valore*
4 – *S'io fosse quelli che d'amor fu' degno*
5 – *Dante, un sospiro messager del core*
6 – *I' vegno 'l giorno a te 'nfinite volte*

Rime di corrispondenza, or epistolary poetry, was common in the *Duecento*. A little less than a third of Cavalcanti's surviving poetry takes this form. Most of these pieces are written to other poets, some to well-known figures of the day, and some have unknown addressees. Many have survived as isolated poems without a known response or an initial request. As a result they are often difficult to appreciate due to a lack of contextual information.

The exchange with Dante is an exception because of the profile of Guido's addressee, and because of the number of sonnets addressed to the same person. At least five, possibly six, surviving sonnets by Cavalcanti were addressed specifically to Dante. 'Vedeste, al mio parere' is almost certainly the first of these, written in response to Dante's 'A ciascun' alma presa', which Cavalcanti's near contemporary tells us he wrote at the age of eighteen, or in 1283. This date may be a fiction, but if so it is not far from the truth. It was probably followed shortly afterwards by a second exchange, since the initial sonnet, Dante's 'Guido, i' vorrei che tu e Lapo ed io', is in a similar vein. But it provokes 'S'io fosse quelli che d'Amor fu degno', in which Cavalcanti is already beginning to distance himself from the idyllic fantasy of love. There follow three other sonnets explicitly addressed to Dante, for which, however, we possess neither a response nor an initiating sonnet, if ever they existed. The first two of these, 'Se vedi Amore, assai ti priego, Dante', and 'Dante, un sospiro messagger del core', are both concerned with discussing a third poet-lover, Lapo, and only the second is included here. Finally there is 'I' vegno 'l giorno a te 'nfinite volte', a poem that with beautiful pathos describes the estrangement between the two friends (though the motives remain tantalisingly vague).[5]

Dante describes near the beginning of the *Vita Nuova* how the first sonnet in our selection, 'Vedeste, al mio parere', was written by his *primo amico* in response to his own sonnet, 'A ciascun' alma presa e gentil core'. Cavalcanti was the dedicatee of the *Vita Nuova*. Not only is he directly referred to on numerous occasions, but his poetic voice lingers behind Dante's own, and the book itself can be read as one side of a dialogue between the two Florentine poets on the meaning and function of poetry. The influence of Cavalcanti on Dante's style is most evident in those poems found in chapters XIII to XVI. In chapter XXIV Dante includes the sonnet, 'Io mi senti' svegliar dentro a lo core', which he explicitly states was addressed to Guido. We can suppose that Cavalcanti was prominent in Dante's mind during the composition of many of the poems from the *Vita Nuova*, and others not included in Dante's anthology but composed at a similar time.[6]

The path Dante follows towards the end of the *Vita Nuova* and beyond will take him some distance from Cavalcanti's own ideas on love and poetry. Scholars have speculated in some detail on a parting of ways, given the awkward references to Dante's *primo amico* in the *Commedia*. Many have tried to outline the history of this famous friendship. In so doing, they often give importance to Cavalcanti's doctrinal canzone 'Donna me prega', and point to philosophical differences between the two. These epistolary sonnets are also important in any attempt to map the growing distance between the two writers. Something of a split can be gleaned from the changing tone across the sonnets, but that is all. Cavalcanti never gathered together or commented on his poetry. The corpus remains unordered and is probably incomplete. It is impossible to make anything more than suppositions concerning this famous friendship.

In previous editions these four sonnets are grouped together at the end of the corpus along with all the *rime di corrispondenza*. It makes perfect sense, however, to place them towards the beginning of this present selection given the thematic and linguistic signs of early composition. Furthermore these sonnets offer an insight into a period of transition from the early style of part 1, where the influence of past models is strong, and part 3, where the characteristics which make up an individual voice are already developed. These poems reveal something of Cavalcanti's friendship with Dante, and suggest the ways in which both writers developed poetically through a mutual process of continual confrontation and stimulation. Finally they offer a valuable example of the genre of epistolary poetry.

3 VEDESTE, AL MIO PARERE, ONNE VALORE

'Vedeste, al mio parere, onne valore' was written in response to 'A ciascun' alma presa e gentil core', in which the unknown writer Dante Alighieri described a dream about love and asked for help in its interpretation. Dante tells readers in chapter III of the *Vita Nuova*: 'A questo sonetto fue risposto da molti e di diverse sentenzie; tra li quali fue risponditore quelli cui io chiamo primo de li miei amici, e disse allora uno sonetto, lo quale comincia:. E questo fue quasi lo principio de l'amistà tra lui e me...' [This sonnet was answered by many, who offered a variety of interpretations; among those who answered was the one I call my best friend, who responded with a sonnet beginning: 'Vedeste, al mio parere, onne valore'. This exchange of sonnets marked the beginning of our friendship]. Dante describes this sonnet exchange as the beginning of an important friendship, but he is more circumspect when talking of Cavalcanti's interpretation of the dream: 'Lo verace giudicio del detto sogno non fue veduto allora per alcuno'.

Cavalcanti is able to deal with the dream analysis in the space of the sestet, though he does not cover all the elements of the vision in 'A ciascun alma' (the meaning of the *drappo*, for example, and the lady's reluctance to eat the dreamer's heart, which were elements of the original dream, are not mentioned). But it is the material in the quatrains which is most interesting, and which possibly endeared the sonnet to Dante. For, here, the narrator launches into a description of the realm of Love as an ideal state devoid of the suffering that would dominate much of Cavalcanti's later poetry.

In its celebration of love 'Vedeste, al mio parere' continued to be echoed in much later chapters of the *Vita Nuova*. At what is possibly the culminating point, chapter XXVI, with its two sonnets in praise of Beatrice, one can't help hearing in the opening line of the second, 'Vede perfettamente onne salute', a direct reminder of Guido, not only in the identical positioning of the verb and adjective, but in the common consonant 'p'. By the end of Dante's *libello*, of course, Love's realm is no longer framed by the dichotomy of dream versus reality, rather it has become a potent spiritual force in this world, as the beautiful first tercet of 'Vede perfettamente onne salute' testifies: 'La vista sua fa onne cosa umile; / e non fa sola sé parer piacente, / ma ciascuna per lei riceve onore'. [The sight of her makes every creature humble, and it not only shows her as lovely but through her every woman is honoured]. But Dante only achieves this by leaving behind the escapist idealism of these early poems and passing through a period of pessimism and *sbigottimento* which owed much to Cavalcanti, as part 3 will show.

Versions exist by Pound (two versions, 1912, and a second, previously unpublished version from the period 1927-31); Rossetti (I – To Dante Alighieri. Sonnet: He interprets Dante's Dream, related in the first Sonnet of the Vita Nuova). There is also a prose translation by Foster and Boyde in *Dante's Lyric Poetry*.

STRUCTURAL NOTE

Correspondence sonnets traditionally required the respondent to use the same rhyme-scheme and rhyme-sounds as the original. This Cavalcanti does: ABBA ABBA CDC CDC. Also of note is the *cobla capfinidas* joining the octet to the sestet:[7] "'l cor ne porta' and 'lo core ne portò'. A further link between the quatrains and sestet is the use of the verb *vedere* in lines 1 and 9.

ANNOTATIONS

Line 1: Vedeste: not simply the verb 'to see', but more broadly 'to experience' (Foster and Boyde vol. 2 26). It echoes the principal verb in the last line of Dante's sonnet, 'appresso gir lo ne vedea piangendo'

[Then I saw him go away weeping]. The verb is in the second person plural, or formally polite inflection, whereas *tu* is used by Cavalcanti in all the other sonnets he addressed to Dante, possibly a further sign that this exchange marked the beginning of their acquaintance.

al mio parere: 'in my opinion'. This is not merely a line filler. It corresponds to the request at line 3 of Dante's sonnet: 'in ciò che mi rescrivan suo parvente' [that each may write back to me what he makes of it].

onne valore: 'every valour', or 'the sum of earthly perfection'. See poem 8 for a discussion of the term **valore**. Pound has 'all things availing' (1912); and 'every valour' (1927). Nelson has 'every power'; Rossetti, 'all worth'; and Foster and Boyde, 'all nobility'.

Lines 1 and 2: the repeated syntactic construction has an emphatic function: 'onne valore', 'tutto gioco', and 'quanto bene'. **Gioco** is not 'game', as in modern Italian, but 'gioia', 'joy'. For **bene** see poem 1, line 14.

Line 3: signor valente: this is Love, who is never directly nominated in the sonnet.

se foste in prova del segnor valente: 'if the love who is your lord is the real Love'.

Line 4: il mondo de l'onore: evoking a world of chivalrous love. Rossetti changes the emphasis of some of these abstract nouns, adding adjectives such as 'righteous', so that in lines 3-4 we find, 'If thou wert in his power who here below / Is honour's righteous lord throughout this earth', continuing in lines 5–6: 'Where evil dies, even there he has his birth, / whose justice out of pity's self doth grow'. Pound, in contrast, has 'Who through sheer honour lords it o'er the world'.

Line 5: poi: 'poiché': 'since'.

vive: Love is still the grammatical subject.

in parte: 'in that place'.

noia: 'vexation'. The word stands in opposition to Love, but Rossetti stretched things somewhat in using 'evil'. The whole line reads literally: 'since he lives there where vexation dies'. Pound uses the word 'baseness': 'He liveth in a place where baseness dieth' (1912), and later, 'Where he dwelleth unease ceaseth amain' (1927).

Line 6: tien ragion: 'where he holds court'.

cassar: '*cassero*': a turret, or more generically the highest and best fortified part of a castle. Nelson has 'And holds council in the turret of the mind'.

Line 7 and 8: Foster and Boyde have 'and so softly does he come during sleep that he takes men's hearts away without pain'.

Line 8: ne: with him.

Line 10: alla morte cadea: the death spoken of here is metaphorical: 'she was falling out of love'. See part 3 where the narrator dies repeatedly at the hands of Love and his lady. Two readings of the manuscript exist here. I have followed De Robertis, who in turn follows Favati. The other version, now found in Cassata, but also adopted by editors previous to Favati, is as follows 'che vostra donna la Morte chedea'. Here the subject is Death, who asks to have for himself the lover's lady. Both Rossetti and Pound follow this second reading. Rossetti, for example, has 'That Death had claim'd thy lady for her prey'.

Line 11: nodriala: 'to give her nourishment'.

di ciò temendo: 'fearful that the lady would die'.

Line 12: se 'n gia dolendo: 'he went away unhappy'.

Line 13: dolce sonno: parallels line 7 **soave per sonno**. Guido seems to be associating Love with a dream, an idea that is developed in poem 4. It is interesting to note the lover's passivity – he can observe, experience and suffer love, but not act upon it.

si compiea: 'was coming to an end'.

Line 14: 'l su' contraro: the opposite of the dream, that is, a state of wakefulness.

4 S'IO FOSSE QUELLI CHE D'AMOR FU' DEGNO

This sonnet was written in response to Dante's poem 'Guido, i' vorrei che tu e Lapo ed io', which we shall need to examine briefly in order to appreciate Cavalcanti's reply. Foster and Boyde coined the expression 'wish-poem' in talking of Dante's sonnet (Foster and Boyde 52). In 'Guido, i' vorrei' Dante's wish was to make a journey by boat with his friends and their ladies, and like its Provençal models the poem includes recourse to the magician Merlin, 'il buono incantatore' [the good wizard]. The first quatrain of Dante's sonnet describes this wish 'vorrei che .../ fossimo presi per incantamento / e messi in un vasel ch'ad ogni vento / per mare andasse, al voler vostro e mio' [I wish .... we could be taken by magic and placed in a boat that, whatever the wind, was carried over the sea wherever you and I chose to go]. The word *incantatore* used to describe Merlin rhymes with 'amore', and contains the root 'canto', song, so that, significantly, poetry, love, and magical escape are all linked. Memorable for its charming optimism and sweetness of expression, Dante's sonnet had taken its spirit and much of its imagery from the anonymous late *Duecento* poem in unrhymed hendecasyllables, *Il mare amoroso*, lines 212-233 in particular, where the similarity is such that one could talk of a condensed translation or imitation: 'E se potesse avere una barchetta, / tal com' fu quella che donò Merlino / ... / ch'andassì ben per terra com' per aqua;/ ... / ... lo vostro cuor d'una sentenza / e d'un volere col mio intendimento' [And if I could have a boat similar to that which Merlin gave as a gift ... that travelled both over land and sea ... and if your heart were one in thought and will with my plan].

Cavalcanti's response is a sophisticated refusal which recalls, in turn, the end of the wish passage in *Il mare amoroso*, summed up in line 234: 'Ma poi ch'i non mi sento tal natura, che faragio?' [But since I do not feel myself to be of such a nature, what should I do?]. Cavalcanti, too, declines because of his own incapacity: 'S'io fosse quelli che d'Amor fu' degno / del qual non trovo sol che rimembranza'. Evidently he is not worthy of Love, since Love only makes him suffer. Indeed Love seems to take pleasure in his suffering, and therefore he feels excluded from that *amoroso regno*. There is an indirect questioning of the idealism of Dante, as Guido asks his friend, as a member of that realm, to judge his dismal situation in love. The idea that to experience love is to suffer unreasonably is a trademark of the poems in part 3.

Versions exist by Pound (1912), Rossetti (IX – To Dante Alighieri. Sonnet: Guido answers the foregoing Sonnet, speaking with shame of his changed Love), and Foster and Boyde.

STRUCTURAL NOTE

Cavalcanti's sonnet follows the rhyme-pattern of the proposition, ABBA ABBA CDE EDC, but adopts different rhyme-sounds. De Robertis points out, however, that the –*io* rhyme in Dante is picked up and turned around in Guido's reply. From a rhyme-sound joining exterior lines in the sestet it becomes interior, and from the masculine it changes to the feminine –*ia*, so that one finds a formal correlation to the radical reversal of the lover's situation that Cavalcanti describes.

ANNOTATIONS

Line 1: S'io fosse quelli: 'Were I still he'. The narrator compares himself to the person he once was and finds hardly any point of similarity. 'Still', in the translation, is inferred in the original's second line, 'del qual non trovo sol che rimembranza', which is, literally, 'of which nothing remains but a memory'. Pound has 'Were I that I that once was worthy of Love'.

d'Amor fu' degno: 'held by Love to be worthy'. This construction emphasises the passivity of the narrator in questions of love: he must depend on the will of Love and his lady.

Line 3: altra sembianza: 'a different countenance'.

Line 4: piaceria: 'piacerebbe', 'I would like'.

legno: synecdoche for 'ship'. It refers to the 'vasel' in Dante's sonnet. Both Rossetti and Pound were using an edition with the erroneous 'segno' in place of 'legno'. This leads to some confusion in their translations: Rossetti, 'To hear this thing might bring me joy thereof', with the pleonastic adverb at the end of the line; Pound, 'Then would this sort of sign please me enough'.

Line 5: E: this conjunction should be read more as 'but' than 'and', for the second quatrain marks something of a change in direction, from a general introduction to a discussion of the predicament of the narrator himself.

amoroso regno: the carefree and optimistic state of Dante's fantasy, and the enchantment, which could overcome every obstacle therein.

Line 6: literally 'there where out of compassion hope is born'. The source of compassion could not be other than the lover's lady.

Line 7: pesanza: a Provençialism for 'sadness' and 'suffering'.

spirito: the person as a whole. Cavalcanti is asking Dante to draw a comparison between their respective situations. The comparison is implicit in the juxtaposition of lines 5-6 with lines 7-8.

riguarda se: 'consider whether'.

Line 8: un prest' arcier: 'a swift archer' is the literal translation, used by both Nelson and Rossetti. I tend to agree with De Robertis, however, who says that it is the lady herself, turned enemy combatant, and no longer the friend and ally happy with Dante's voyage. This seems more plausible than the possibility that the archer is a rival lover. Pound is somewhat astray in lines 7-8 with 'Judge as thou canst from my dim mood's distress / What bowman and what target are concerned'. The riddle to be solved, if 'riguarda' of line 7 is to be read as a similar invitation to that which Dante made in 'A ciascun alma presa', lies not in the identity of the 'arcier' but rather in the 'maraviglia' of the last tercet. I have used 'an archeress' in order to suggest the narrator's lady should be intended.

Line 9: tragge: 'shot'.

tese: 'gave'. A literal translation would be 'she fires the bow [arrow] which Love had given her'. The emphasis of the elaborate construction is on the complicity between Love and the lady. Pound writes 'Straining his arc, behold Amor the bowman', despite the original clearly describing the bow being handed over by Love to the **arcier**. Strangely enough, Rossetti, whom Pound nearly always follows on questions of interpretation, is much more accurate: 'For a swift archer, whom his [Love's] feats approve, / Now bends the bow, which Love to him did yield'. Foster and Boyde have 'for a ready archer has made it his target, and shoots from the bow which Love strung for him so cheerfully that he appears entirely joyful'.

Line 10: lietamente: 'gaily', or without giving thought to the consequences for the lover.

la sua persona: 'she herself'.

Line 11: gioco: 'joy', as in poem 3, line 2.

porti signoria: 'is mistress of, or in full possession of, joy'. Lines 10-11 are difficult to translate. A literal version might run, 'so happily, that she herself / seems to be the lord of joy'. Rossetti interprets the passage quite differently in translating, 'In such mere sport against me it would seem / As though he held his lordship for a jest'. Pound is somewhat clearer when he writes, 'Draweth so gaily that to see his face / You'd say he held his rule for merriment'. Nelson interprets the passage with Pound, but De Robertis' reading, for which the lady herself is the archeress, again proves to be much more coherent.

Line 12: odi maraviglia: the emphasis is on the inexplicable nature of what the narrator is about to say.

el disia: 'that he desires'. I take the subject to be the narrator's spirit, though it could equally be the 'prest' arcier'. I can see no reason why the archer should desire an extraordinary thing and why the reader should be interested, whereas it is quite consistent with Cavalcanti that the spirit, in love, desires what destroys it. Pound and Rossetti followed erroneous originals here. Rossetti possibly read 'ria' in the place of 'disia' to arrive at 'sorriest': 'Then hear the marvel which is sorriest'; while Pound read 'ch'ella fia' to arrive at the equally banal 'to all intent': 'Yet hear what's marvellous in all intent'.

Line 13: fedito: 'ferito'.

li: 'a lei': forgives her (the lover's lady).

Line 14: the contradiction is implicit in the original. De Robertis rightly reads 'benché veda' for **vedendo**: 'even though he sees'. Nelson maintains the original construction, and uses the present participle in his translation: 'seeing that he destroys its strength'. But in his version the force of the paradox is almost lost.

valore: here the meaning is somewhat different to poem 1, line 9, and poem 3, line 1. Vital energy, endurance, power, and potential are all implied in its meaning. Rossetti has 'My sorely wounded soul forgiveth him [the archer], / Yet knows that in his act her [the soul's] strength is kill'd'. Pound's version of the last two lines is: 'The smitten spirit pardoneth his foeman / Which pardon doth that foeman's power debase'.

5 DANTE, UN SOSPIRO MESSAGGER DEL CORE

A number of the poems exchanged between Cavalcanti and Dante make reference to a third lover, Lapo. This is most likely Lapo Gianni, another Florentine stilnovo poet.[8] He is referred to in Dante's invitation 'Guido, io vorrei', and again in two sonnets by Cavalcanti, the present poem and a fifth poem by Cavalcanti addressed to Dante but not included in this selection, 'Se vedi Amore, assai ti priego, Dante'. In that poem Guido questions whether Lapo is really a lover in Love's court, and asks Dante to speak with Love to clear things up. In the present poem it is Cavalcanti who goes to speak with Love on behalf of Lapo. Lapo is referred to indirectly as ''l servidore / di monna Lagia', the servant of Lady Lagia (Lady Lagia we know to be Lapo's lady from Dante's initial poem of invitation).

The poem opens with a dream concerning Love. Although Guido seems to wake in line 3, the tone of the whole poem and the events related have a dream-like quality similar to Dante's 'A ciascun'alma presa e gentil core'. Take, for example, the awkward temporal and spatial shift from the first to the second quatrain. One wonders whether the appearance of Lapo and the encounter with Love are not a continuation of the initial dream, or at least a vision experienced in a state of drowsiness, or whether, in fact, the initial lines concern a dream within a dream. The theme of Love communicating through dreams was not uncommon. It occurs again in the opening lines of the sonnet Dante says he sent to Cavalcanti in the *Vita Nuova* XXIV, 'Io mi senti' svegliar dentro a lo core / un spirito amoroso che dormia: / e poi vidi venir da lungi Amore / allegro sì, che appena il conoscea' ['I felt a sleeping spirit of love awaken in my heart, and then I saw Love coming from far off, so joyful that I hardly knew him']. In Dante's poem there are many lexical and thematic links with the first four lines of the present sonnet, not least of which are the common positions of *core* and a form of the verb *dormire* at the end of the first two lines.

Versions exist by Pound (1912) and Rossetti (X – To Dante Alighieri. Sonnet: He reports, in a feigned Vision, the successful Issue of Lapo Gianni's Love).

STRUCTURAL NOTE
This sonnet has the same rhyme scheme, ABBA ABBA CDE EDC, as both the previous and the following poems.

ANNOTATIONS
Line 1: sospiro messagger del core: 'a sigh arising from the heart'. The personification of the sigh is typical of the dramatic atmosphere so common in Cavalcanti. Common, also, is the use of the term 'messenger' to describe this process. Personified feelings and psyco-physical responses in the shape of spirits, as well as abstract nouns like Love, and even the poems themselves, often act as go-betweens. As a result the I of the narrator is always slightly distant from the centre of things and lacks control over this chain of communication.
Line 2: subitamente: 'suddenly'.
dormendo: 'while I was sleeping'.
Line 4: e': the sigh of line 1.
non fosse in compagnia d'Amore: Guido fears that the sigh is accompanied by Love. The presence of Love was often an overwhelming experience for the lover. Fear at Love's sudden arrival, and the adverb subitamente, are both found in Dante's dream poem 'A ciascun' alma presa e gentil core'. In the second quatrain there is a temporal shift. Guido sees his friend Lapo (the servant of Lady Lagia). The implication seems to be that the initial sigh relats to Lapo, not Guido. In this case it is not clear why the sigh is a messenger from

Guido's own heart, unless as a fellow lover and friend he is in tune with Lapo's predicament. Such details can best be explained by the dream-like quality of the poem dicussed above.

non: In Latin the negative was used after verbs expressing fear, without necessarily indicating a negative. So Guido feared the sigh *was* accompanied by Love. A similar construction is found in poem 14, lines 1-2.

Lines 5-6: vidi 'l servitore / di monna Lagia: this servant in love, as we know from Dante's sonnet 'Guido i' vorrei che tu e Lapo ed io', is Lapo Gianni.

Line 8: i' presi di merzé tanto valore: 'I drew such strength from my feeling of compassion'. A circumlocution for Guido's sense of compassion. Rossetti has 'So much of Pity's essence entered me'.

Line 9: giunsi: 'came before'. Nelson has 'caught up with'; Pound, 'found'; Rossetti, 'I was ware of Love'.

Amore ch'affilava i dardi: such incidental detail is not common in Cavalcanti. The threatening image of Love fits with the narrator's fear in the first quatrain.

Line 10: I asked Love about Lapo's [**su'**] suffering.

Line 12: servente: this is Lapo. The lady is his lady, monna Lagia.

prisa: 'captured'. That is, she has fallen in love with Lapo, and therefore he need not worry.

Line 13: su' piacimento: in opposition to the parallel construction **Su' tormento** in line 10.

Line 14: di' ch'a li occhi guardi: 'tell him to observe his lady's eyes'.

6 *I' VEGNO 'L GIORNO A TE 'NFINITE VOLTE*

The final sonnet in our selection of those addressed to Dante is famous for relating to a rupture between the two friends. The details of this rift remain obscure, and the present sonnet offers no more than tantalising suggestions as to a solution. It is best read as a peace missive. The tone is more personal than that of the previous three sonnets, even where it describes a new coolness between the friends. Branca suggests that despite the tension created by a difference of opinion, one senses an underlying closeness which charges the poem with pathos.

The reasons why Cavalcanti now finds Dante's behaviour or attitude unfavourable, or why he is concerned for his depressed state, as the case may be, is still an issue for debate, but it is also practically unsolvable. Many propositions exist.[9] They depend principally on whether the key adjective used to describe Dante, *vile*, 'low', is seen to indicate a state of depression in Dante (Contini suggests discouragement, 'scoraggiamento', as a modern equivalent to express this interpretation), or to refer to Dante having acted ignobly. Following the first line of interpretation, an obvious reason for depression in Dante could be the death of Beatrice.[10] If ignobility is intended then some commentators point to Dante's attraction to the 'donna gentile' (Contini); or the feud with Forese (Branca); or a falling out between the two poets motivated either philosophically,[11] or politically.[12] A further proposition is that Love personified addresses Dante in the sonnet (De Robertis).

My own opinion is that Cavalcanti himself addresses Dante in the sonnet, following a rupture between the two based on some family or political difference for which Dante would be to some extent responsible. If one considers the way in which the sonnet describes Dante, it becomes apparent that the emphasis is on problems stemming from social relations: from one who was disdainful of people, 'Solevanti spiacer persone molte', who in human relationships would not compromise his values, 'tuttor fuggivi l'annoiosa gente'; he has now become, by contrast, 'vile', either depressed or ignoble. 'Vile' recurs thrice, each time in reference to a different aspect of Dante's person: 'pensar vilmente', in relation to thought or the mind; 'la vil tua vita', life; and 'l'anima invilita', the soul. In contrast to 'vile', Cavalcanti employs the expressions 'gentil tua mente' and 'tue vertù'.

While the first quatrain remains generic, the second is slightly more specific in its references to a social context: 'persone molte' and 'annoiosa gente', and 'parlav'. In the sestet this current continues. Cavalcanti doesn't dare to appear before Dante now. But he continues to think of his friend and does communicate through poetry with a fond and eager spirit. The emphasis in words like 'mostramento', 'guisa', and even 'vita' seems to be on the public status of Dante, as if Cavalcanti was restrained from acknowledging Dante by an external force. This suggests that the differences between them cannot be reduced to Dante's depression, and are to be found in a socio-political context, rather than in a personal, poetical or philosophical sphere. Indeed Cavalcanti continues to evoke poetry as a common bond. He suggests as a remedy for Dante's degraded state the frequent reading of the present sonnet, as if its recital could act as a prayer or form of penitence to the God of poetry and nobility to drive out the evil spirits and the transient affairs of family and state.

Finally whatever the details of the tension, it is important to keep in mind the conciliatory tone of the present sonnet. The sophisticated and, ultimately, playful spirit evokes the common fraternity of poetry, and could not be further from the more polemical rupture found in Cavalcanti's sonnet addressed to Guittone, 'De più a uno face un sollegismo'.

Versions exist by Pound (1912) and Rossetti (XX – To Dante Alighieri. Sonnet: He rebukes Dante for his way of Life, after the Death of Beatrice). There is also a translation by Percy Bysshe Shelley.[13] Shelley's version is in regular iambic pentameters and rhymes ABBA CDCD EFE FGG, though he makes frequent recourse to assonance in place of rhyme.

STRUCTURAL NOTE

The structure of the poem is intricate. One needs to look beyond the sonnet form and rhyme scheme (ABBA ABBA CDE EDC) to appreciate the subtlety and playfulness inherent. Firstly both rhyme-sounds in the quatrains finish with the syllable –te, which, not by chance, is a second person singular pronoun. In fact the syllable is found throughout the sonnet, not only as the eleventh metrically relevant syllable. There are frequent alliterations in t: at least two words in each line begin with t, making forty-eight t's altogether, and there are thirteen second person singular personal pronouns and possessive adjectives. The opening line is an excellent example: '*te*' with tonic accent found in sixth position, then repeated atonically in positions 9 and 11; a parallel is discernible with the fourth line which, as well as sharing the same rhyme-sound, has its principal tonic accent in sixth position, '*-tù*', followed by a secondary accent, '*ti*' in eighth position. The second quatrain, which shares with the first a binary division, also reveals internal parallels: the external lines, 5 and 8, have tonic accents in second and sixth position, while the internal two lines are both *a minore* with atonic fifth '*-vi*' and '*-v'i*''. Similarly in the tercets: lines 9 and 10 are *a minore* with tonic accent on the eighth metrically relevant syllable; lines 12 and 13 are *a maiore* with secondary tonic accents on the third and second respectively; and the closing line of each tercet is *a minore* with a secondary tonic accent in sixth position. The opening lines of each tercet share the following peculiarity: in line 9 all three of its tonic accents (principal and secondary) contain the vowel *i*; while in line 12 the tonic syllables all contain the vowel *e*.

ANNOTATIONS

Line 1: literally the original reads, 'I come to you infinite times a day'. One imagines that this is done through the process of thinking. However advocates of the interpretation which sees Love as the narrator point to a literal reading of this line to strengthen their argument. Shelley has 'Returning from its daily quest, my Spirit'. There are numerous echoes in Shakespeare. See sonnets CXIII, 'Since I left you mine eye is in my mind'; and XXX, 'When to the sessions of sweet silent thought' with its final couplet, 'But if the while I think on thee, dear friend, / All losses are restored and sorrows end'.

'l giorno: is not, as Rossetti and Nelson have translated, 'by daytime' or 'during the day', which would seem to indicate a dichotomy with night, but rather 'daily'.

Line 2: 'and I find you thinking in too lowly a manner'.

vilmente: Pound uses 'vilely', Shelley uses 'vile', and the other English translators use a form of 'base'. The root *vile* occurs thrice in the sonnet. In meaning it is still close to the Latin *vilem, vilis*: 'of low value, common, mean, base'. It could range in meaning from 'of low social rank' to 'lacking in intellectual qualities and spiritual nobility'. In this second ambit it is often found in Cavalcanti and Dante in opposition to *nobile*. But it is not limited to the English 'vile', meaning of despicable moral behaviour, or physically repulsive. 'Depressed', as we saw above, could also be a possible meaning in this context, as could 'lacking in courage', or, perhaps, 'not willing to take responsibility for one's own actions.

Line 3: **gentil tua mente**: *gentile* was frequently found in conjunction with *nobile*. Both adjectives suggest the idea of Love as an improving force. See poem 1 for a discussion of *gentile*. That it is found here with **mente** suggests a nobility of mind. One also finds *vile* in opposition to *gentile* in poem 17, lines 4 –5; and poem 20, lines 8-9. Pound translates, 'thy noble mind / And virtue's plenitude'. This is similar to Shelley, 'thy mild and gentle mind / Those ample virtues'; and Rossetti, 'thy gentle mind / And for thy many virtues'.

Line 4: **ti son tolte**: 'have been taken away from you'. Despite the accusations of *viltà*, the tone of the sonnet remains at all times respectful and communicates deep affection, partly by making Dante passive at crucial points such as here.

Line 5: **persone molte**: 'multitudes of people'. Most likely a euphemism for 'you were very careful in your choice of company'.

Line 6: **l'annoiosa gente**: not 'boring people', but rather, in a courtly sphere, 'the malicious and invidious'. Dante used to shun these people according to the poem. The implication is that he now entertains them. Nelson adopts 'tiresome'. Pound uses 'rabble'. Rossetti has 'It was thy wont to shun much company, / Unto all sorry concourse ill inclined'. Shelley has 'Once thou didst loathe the multitude / Of blind and madding men'.

Line 7: I have preferred Cassata's version of the original, **di te parlav'i'**, over the reading of Favati, and De Robertis who have 'di me parlavi'. The problem, of course, is that in the only two existing manuscripts of this poem, both from some time after Cavlacanti, the scribe uses no punctuation and no spaces between words, so that it appears 'dimeparlavi'. De Robertis follows what he calls the sound philological rule of not altering the text in order to suit a specific interpretation, and in theory I would have no hesitation in agreeing with him. But in this case the sense of the line is nothing less than puzzling when one reads 'di me parlavi': 'you spoke of me with such warmth of heart / that I welcomed all your poetry'. Mutual back scratching is a strange activity to mention in the context of celebrating a friendship. Furthermore, as Cassata says, the use of 'fuggivi' in the previous line, and the emphatic use of *'te'* throughout the sonnet, could easily have led to an error on the part of the scribe. All the other English translators follow Favati's reading.

Line 8: avìe: 'avevo', I had.

ricolte: 'Welcomed', or 'thought favourably upon'. Nelson uses 'garnered' which seems a little anachronistic. His version of lines 7-8 is representative of all the other English translations in making Cavalcanti's welcome of Dante's rhymes dependant on his friend praising him: 'You would speak about me with such deep feeling / That I had garnered all your poems'. Shelley strays from the original in these lines. It is not clear if this was a result of a corrupt Italian edition or a deliberate ploy to avoid the difficulty of interpretation, but it seems to work in spirit: 'I then loved thee - / I loved thy lofty songs and that sweet mood / When thou wert faithful to thyself and me'.

Line 9: Or': this adverb introduces an emphatic change of time.

vil tua vita: an ambiguous expression. Nelson has 'your base life', privileging the moral dimension of the term *vile*; Rossetti, 'But now I dare not, for thine abject life'; Shelley, 'thy degraded state'.

Line 10: far mostramento: 'make open sign of', surely in the public sphere, given that the poem itself is already a private sign of affection. Pound has 'To give the sign that thy speech pleaseth me'. But I tend to favour Nelson, who has 'I do not dare / Let on that I like your words'.

Line 11: né 'n guisa vegno a te che tu mi veggi: the verb *venire* is repeated from the opening line. The poet makes a distinction between coming in thought, line 1, and coming in person here. It is interesting to reflect that the sonnet itself acts as a go-between, declaring the first action and explaining how the second is impossible.

Lines 12-14: there is a wonderful change of tone in this closing tercet. One can detect an increased playfulness with the suggestion that the recital of the poem may exorcise the ignoble spirit which holds Dante.

Line 12: presente sonetto: 'the present poem', but perhaps in so far as it is representative of poetry in general.

Line 13: lo spirito noioso: the adjective is repeated from line 6; the spirit is a personification of that vileness which holds Dante, thereby removing him from much of the blame.

'ti caccia: 'pursues you'. Pound picks up the hunting image, and is rather carried away, 'That malign spirit which so hunteth thee / Will sound forloyn and spare thy affrighted soul', printing a gloss for 'forloyn' 'The recall of the hounds'.

Line 14: anima invilita: Nelson translates 'abased soul', thereby using a form of the root 'base' in the three instances in which **vile** appears in the original. Pound has 'affrighted soul'; Rossetti, 'dishonour'd soul'; and Shelley, 'so the false spirit shall fly / And leave to thee thy true integrity'.

PART THREE: LOVE AS *SBIGOTTIMENTO*

7 – *Deh, spiriti miei, quando mi vedete*
8 – *L'anima mia vilment'è sbigotita*
9 – *Tu m'hai sì piena di dolor la mente*
10 – *Io non pensava che lo cor giammai*
11 – *Poi che di doglia cor conven ch'i' porti*
12 – *Perché non fuoro a me gli occhi dispenti*
13 – *Quando di morte mi conven trar vita*
14 – *Io temo che la mia disaventura*

This is the largest of the seven parts into which the present selection from Cavalcanti's poetry has been divided. It contains more poems because it attempts to represent the dominant theme found in his corpus. Broadly speaking one might describe that theme as follows: Love is portrayed as a destructive force able to disrupt the psycho-physical world of the rational being, thus causing *sbigottimento* in the lover. In all of these compositions there is a desire to document the narrator's emotional state. First person pronouns predominate in many opening lines. One cannot help but be struck by the bitter and sometimes aggressive nature of the narrative voices. Cavalcanti's lover is haughty, and has a recriminatory attitude towards Love and his lady. This is evident even where the narrator pleads directly to the lady to be requited, such as in poems 9 and 12.

The term *sbigottimento* is a key word for Cavalcanti. *Sbigottimento* and its cognates are found on eight occasions throughout his poetry. This number is almost equal to the word's total representation in all other *Duecento* poets. It is used to express the severe shock and bewilderment of the lover, and his incapacity to act, as if he were stunned by the force of the experience of love. At the same time the term conveys a sense of alarm and panic. It is by no means a positive state of being; hence it is associated with *vilmente* in its appearance in the first line of poem 8, 'L'anima mia vilmente è sbigotita'. In part 3 it occurs in poems 7 and 8, and twice in poem 10, but it describes the state of being common to all these pieces. It also appears in poem 20, and both poems in part 7, poems thematically close to these in many ways.

Personification is one of the rhetorical techniques used by Cavalcanti to express the lover's *sbigottimento*, and the poems in part 3 are characterised by the prosopopoeia of various internal psycho-physical elements. The eyes, the heart, the soul, the mind, and the spirits are principal characters. They often express opposing states of being, or emotions, leading to a situation of dramatic tension.

A second rhetorical technique adopted to convey *sbigottimento* is that of antithesis. Poem 13 is the best example, for the entire ballad is structured around a series of opposites and oxymorons. The opening of poem 11 is structured in a similar way.

7 DEH, SPIRITI MIEI, QUANDO MI VEDETE

This is an excellent poem to open part 3 because it is something of a transition between the early sonnets of praise and the more recriminatory tone of what follows. The narrator addresses his own spirits. He asks them to act as intermediaries, in order both to express pain and to console the suffering of his mind, heart, and soul. The repeated interjection, *Deh*, like a sigh of resignation, contributes to the quieter, more intimate atmosphere of suffering.

Rossetti published no version of this sonnet. There is one translation by Pound, published in 1912.

STRUCTURAL NOTE
The rhyme scheme for this sonnet is ABBA ABBA CDC CDD. In line 1 *vedete* did indeed rhyme with the other A rhymes. It is a so-called Sicilian rhyme because it derived from the practice of the Sicilian poets, who immediately preceded the generation of Cavalcanti, to rhyme the closed

vowel *e* as *i* in such situations. It is not a common feature in Cavalcanti and soon disappears from standard practice. There is a close link between rhymes A and B. The structural balance afforded by the rhymes is reinforced by grammatical links in the quatrains: the outer two lines (lines 1-2 and 7-8) have rhyme words which are second person plural verbs, while those of the four internal lines are plural adjectives. The poem is further structured around the interjection *Deh*, which opens lines 1, 5, 7 and 12.

ANNOTATIONS

Line 1: **Deh:** an interjection that can express anything from surprise to disappointment and despair. The second two words would seem to be more fitting in this context. But the word does contribute to the quieter feeling of heartache when compared to the energetic and aggressive suffering of the two poems immediately following this one. Nelson uses 'Ah' in the first instance and then 'Alas' in the following three. Pound has 'Alas' twice, then "Las!' and then 'Woe!'. In repetition the word reinforces the sense of stasis and passivity in the narrator.

spiriti: refer to the introduction for a discussion of this term.

Line 2: **come:** here an interogative, 'why'. As is the case with other poems in part 3, the opening phrase is a question which underlines the narrator's own despair and passivity.

Lines 2-3: the spirits would seem to be necessary in order to convey words from the mind to the external world.

Line 4: **sbigottite:** for a discussion of this term see the introduction to part 3. It is a difficult term to translate. Nelson has 'dismayed', Pound, 'deep distress'.

Line 6: **di:** 'caused by'. The heart's wounds are caused by three things: the image of the woman (*sguardo*), her beauty (*piacere*), and her benevolence (*umiltate*), a trinity which is echoed in the woman's three qualities in line 10 (Contini).

Line 8: **vertù:** not moral qualities, but the heart's faculties, or life spirits.

Nelson has 'powers'; Pound, 'power-stripped, naked, confounded'. The word is repeated in line 11.

Lines 9-11: the first tercet is little more than a variation on what we have just been told about the heart in the second quatrain.

Line 9: luï: the pronoun refers to the heart.

spirito: this spirit which appears before the heart is not to be confused with the narrator's own spirits. It is, rather, an image of the beloved woman that enters the narrator and causes *sbigottimento*. But a link does exist between this spirit and the spirits of the narrator, since it is these latter that transmit the image to the heart.

Line 10: gentile: 'noble'. See poem 1, line 2.

Line 12: the first hemistich is identical to that of line 7.

deggiate dire: a phrasiological verb with greater rhetorical force for 'say'. Nelson has 'I beg you kindly to tell'.

Line 14: ella: the soul.

fie: 'sarà'.

8 *L'ANIMA MIA VILMENT'È SBIGOTITA*

This sonnet concerns the narrator's turbulent emotional state as a result of love. Much of the imagery and lexicon are taken from the sphere of war, and for this Cavalcanti cannot have avoided the influence of Guinizzelli, who had described Love entering into the lover like the storming of an opposing army: 'Amor m'assale e già non ha reguardo' [Love assaults me and still is unconcerned] ('Lo vostro bel saluto'); and 'Ed io dal suo valor son assalito / con sì fera battaglia di sospiri' [And I am struck by her indwelling worth / In such a wild battle of sighs] ('Veduto ho la lucente stella diana'). In the midst of the Cavalcantian phase of the *Vita Nuova* one finds similar imagery: 'Questa battaglia d'Amore' [This battle of Love], for example, in chapter XVI, 4; and again in the sonnet 'Ciò che m'incontra nella mente more', in chapter XV.

Rossetti published no translation of poem 8. Pound's translation is from 1912.

STRUCTURAL NOTE

This sonnet is unique in Cavalcanti, and in all the *Duecento*, in having the rhyme scheme ABBB BAAA CDD DCC. The lack of symmetry reflects the speaker's own internal confusion. But it is no less skilfully crafted for that. The two rhyme-sounds in the quatrains, *-ore* and *–ita*, contain the two poles of *more* and *vita*, while the first quatrain contains the three central elements of the poem in rhyme: *core*, *amore*, and *more* (Contini).

There is little evidence of thematic progression in this sonnet. The tercets offer a repetition rather than a development of theme and key words in the quatrains. The first tercet describes the process by which Love conquered the lover. This had already been set out in the opening quatrain, which also makes use of the word 'battaglia'. Likewise the second tercet repeats elements of the second quatrain, namely the hypothetical construction using the principal verb *vedere*. Any linear thematic development has been disrupted as the narrator dwells obsessively on his emotional state.

ANNOTATIONS

Line 1: **vilment'**: see poem 4 for a discussion of this term. Two interpretations of the adverb seem possible here. In the first the soul is reduced to a state of misery. In the second the narrator's soul is shaken due to the vileness of the agent. Pound suggests the second alternative in his construction, 'So vilely is this soul of mine confounded'. But there is no suggestion in the original that *vilmente* should be associated with that moral depravity conveyed by the English 'vile'. Nelson is more literally correct, 'My soul is abjectly appalled'.

sbigotita: It is difficult to find an English equivalent for all the shades of meaning in this word. Pound avoids it. Nelson has 'appalled'. Cirigliano has 'terrified'.

Line 2: *ave dal core*: *ave* is literally 'has'. The soul was said to reside in the heart. The suggestion is that the heart is under siege from a foreign army. In line 6 the soul is forced to abandon the castle and flee. Pound has misinterpreted the entire quatrain. He has disassociated the lover's predicament from the assault made by Love. It is difficult to imagine why, and the result is confused: 'So vilely is this soul of mine confounded / By strife grown audible within the heart / That if toward her some frail Love but start / With unaccustomed speed, she swoons astounded'.

Line 3: ella: the soul. I have maintained the Italian gender of the various internal organs in the translation for sake of clarity.

Line 4: più presso a lui che non sòle: 'closer to him [the heart] than at present, or than is usual'. A literal translation of lines 3 and 4 might run, 'that if she [the soul] feels Love [come] even a little / closer to him [the heart] than at present, she will die'. The presence of Love in the narrator is already so strong that if Love gains any more ground in the heart the soul will die.

Lines 5-8: In this second quatrain the soul, in order to avoid immanent death has fled the heart. The two past participles in rhyme emphasise this point. The passage from the first to the second quatrain is awkward and does not appear to show a logical progression, though this is somewhat masked by the perfunctory comparison in line 5 and the hypothetical construction in lines 7-8.

Line 5: the subject is still the soul.

valore: 'life-force'. The word is common in both Cavalcanti and, particularly, Dante, who imbues it with a range of meanings, including 'goodness' and 'nobility'. Here it is clearly used to refer to the strength, resilience, and vital force of the lover. The connection between vital energy and life is evidenced in the parallel constructions at the end of the fifth and eighth lines: 'non ha valore' and 'non ha vita'.

Line 8: questi: most probably refers to the lover, though it could also indicate the heart. Pound read *questa* here, leading him to maintain the soul as the subject of the line, 'Would deem her one whom death's sure cloak surroundeth'.

Line 9: Per li occhi: the eyes were the path Love took, in the form of an image of the beloved object, to reach the lover's heart. Guinizzelli, for example, opens the tercets of 'Lo vostro bel saluto' with 'per li occhi passa' [enters through the eyes], and a look at the opening lines of Cavalcanti's fifty-two extant poems reveals the word 'occhi' on nine occasions, including in poem 12, 'Perché non fuoro a me gli occhi dispenti'.

Line 10: **immantenente**: 'immediately'.

Line 12: 'whoever is he who most happiness feels', and therefore, 'Even the happiest man in the world ... could not help but weep in pity'.

Line 13: the **spiriti** are the vital spirits.

Lines 13-14: the original is not clear. Are the 'spirits' and the possessive adjective, 'sua', those of the lover, or of the happiest man? I have followed De Robertis who claims they refer to the happiest man. It is equally possible, however, that the spirits are those of the narrator, for whom the happiest person weeps in pity. This is the interpretation favoured by Pound, who has 'Whoe'er he be who holdeth joy most close / would, should he see my spirit going hence, / weep for the pity and make no pretense'. The idea of evoking compassion and pity, linked to the demonstration of suffering, recurs frequently in Cavalcanti. If that were the case here, however, one would have expected to find not 'the happiest person', but rather 'the most self-absorbed'. Nelson leaves the English ambiguous when he translates, 'If he should but see the spirits take flight, / He would weep out of his great pity'.

Line 14: **pietate**: either 'pity' or 'suffering', depending on whether one follows Pound or De Robertis respectively.

9 *TU M'HAI SÌ PIENA DI DOLOR LA MENTE*

This is one of Cavalcanti's most dramatically charged poems. It is addressed directly to the lover's lady, who is accused of being the cause of his suffering. Once again such suffering is catalogued in detail. In the first quatrain each line is dedicated to one of the unruly subjects, 'la mente', 'l'anima', ''l cor', and the 'occhi', all of whom serve to show how little control the narrator has over himself.

The sestet contains the comparison of the narrator with a statue. It is interesting to compare this image with its source in Guinizzelli's sonnet 'Lo vostro bel saluto': 'Rimango come statua di ottono / ove spirito, né vita non ricorre, / se non che la figura d'uomo rende'. [I stand quietly like a brass statue / with no life or spirit flowing, / filling out the bare shape of a man]. Cavalcanti's reworking places a greater emphasis on the faculty of sight, and deceptive visual appearance. It is not until the enjambement leading into line 11 that the reader encounters the statue. As De Robertis notes, the frequent use of expressions such as *come, che pare* all point to the extremity of the paradox and the difficulty of expressing it: the lover is dead and yet lives and suffers still. Furthermore the ending of the sonnet pushes Guinizzelli's image one step further, irreverently suggesting at a link between the statue and the figure of the martyr.

There is no version by Rossetti, and one by Pound (1912).

STRUCTURAL NOTE

The rhyme scheme of this sonnet is the less common form generally associated with Cavalcanti's early poetry, ABAB ABAB CDE DCE. The thematic similarity to the previous sonnet is strengthened by the repetition here of three rhyme-endings from 'L'anima mia vilment'è sbigotita', A, C and D. 'Tu' opens the poem, 'Amor' opens the second quatrain, and 'I'' opens the sestet.

ANNOTATIONS

Lines 1: **Tu**: the lady is addressed with the familiar *tu* form, whereas in other of Cavlacanti's poems, such as poem 23, she is addressed with the formal *voi*. Cassata has suggested that one may use this as a clue to ordering the poems, on the basis of a growing familiarity between the narrator and his lady which would see a change from *voi* to *tu* at some stage (Cassata). This seems unlikely. Certainly any increased familiarity here has also led to an increase in suffering. The pronoun which opens the sonnet almost bursts onto the page, such is the force and pressure of the pain that the invective tries to alleviate. Pound adopts 'Thou' in his version, 'Thou fill'st my mind with griefs so populous'.

m'hai sì piena di dolor la mente: Nelson offers a good literal version of this line, 'you have my mind so filled with sorrow'.

Line 2: si briga: 'calculates how' (Contini). Nelson's use of 'contrives' seems appropriate, 'That my soul contrives to depart'. Pound has 'That my soul irks him to be on the road'. As in the previous sonnet, the soul, which normally resides in the heart, is tempted to flee out of fear and shock. The image of the lifeless statue in the sestet is an extension of the idea of a body without soul and life-force.

Line 3: the **sospiri** or 'sighs' are an expression of the suffering of the heart. The heart sends them out (*manda*) in this case.

Line 4: mostrano: the sighs become visible signs of the heart's suffering by turning into tears. Cassata, however, favours an alternative manuscript which reads *dicono*, in place of *mostrano* here.

Line 5: tuo grande valor sente: while **valore** was used in the previous sonnet to describe the narrator's own life-force, here, in describing the lady, the meaning is closer to 'worth, virtue and nobility'. Pound has 'Love, sensitive to thy nobility'; Nelson, 'Love, that senses your great power'.

Line 6: Amor...dice: Love acts as a go-between who is sympathetic to the lover, whereas in the previous sonnet there was little distinction drawn between Love and the lady.

ti convien morire: 'you must die'. The love-death relationship is discussed further in 'Donna me prega', line 35, 'Di sua potenza segue spesso morte'. Various levels of meaning may be at play, and Cavalcanti is not concerned to limit our understanding to a literal death, or a sensation of lifelessness, or the moral death which Dante discusses in *Convivio*, IV, vii, 14, 'Morte è colui che non segue la ragione' [Dead is he who does not live by reason].

Line 7: fiera donna: literally 'fierce lady'. Nelson has 'cruel'. I have changed the construction slightly to 'such a lady'. There is a dispute as to whether the adjective, **fiera**, is correct anyway, since Cassata follows an alternative codex which has *bella*. Pound was also using this version of the original, and consequently he writes 'this fair lady'.

Line 8: gaining pity, mercy and compassion from the lady was an important step in the process of love. It gave the lover the strength to continue suffering patiently, in the hope that his patience would be rewarded at a later date.

Line 9: I' vo come colui ch': literally 'I am like one who...'.

Line 10: a chi lo sguarda: 'to whoever observes him'.

Line 12: che si conduca: 'conducts himself, carries on'. Nelson's 'That can walk only by artifice' narrows the range of meaning.

Maestria: 'artifice'.

Lines 13-14: the **ferita** (wound) is an **aperto segno** (visible sign) which explains how the lover met his death. It is not coincidental that the martyr, too, was traditionally represented as a statue ostending the method of his or her martyrdom (witness Santa Lucia holding her eyes, for example). The ostension of the heart seems to suggest, quite irreverently, that the lover is a martyr to the god of Love. The idea returns in the tercets of poem 12.

10 *IO NON PENSAVA CHE LO COR GIAMMAI*

Cavalcanti wrote only two surviving canzoni of more than one stanza. While the other, 'Donna me prega', is widely known, the present poem is less familar, particularly to English readers. Despite its greater length, it is closely linked to the poems of *sbigottimento*. In the first stanza the now common effects of love on the narrator are described. The middle two stanzas then explain why Cavalcanti has so much trouble contemplating his lady and describing her in words. Stanza 3 is really a variation on stanza 2, rather than a progression, and even repeats a key phrase ('quand' eo penso bene' and 'Quando 'l pensier mi vèn'). Such repetition is not a sign of clumsiness. On the contrary, circling around an idea or theme while varying the angle from which it is approached was a common structural technique in early Italian poetry.[14]

It was also common for the concluding stanza of a canzone to be addressed directly to the poem itself. The narrator would give final instructions before sending it out into the world. This leave-taking was known as a *congedo*. The final stanza of the present poem is no exception. Its metaphor of the book of Love was to find important echoes in Dante.

There is no version of this poem by Rossetti. This is one of two poems not translated by Pound (the other is the early ballad 'Fresca rosa novella'). According to Anderson, 'Pound was inclined to admit them to the canon, but he did not think them particularly interesting or important, and he did not translate them' (193).

Structural Note

This canzone has four fourteen-line stanzas. All lines are hendecasyllables, except for the second and fifth lines of the sirima, which are *settenari*. The rhyme scheme is ABBC BAAC DeD FeF. Stanzas 2, 3 and 4 all have a passage in direct speech at or close to their conclusion. The word *morte*, or one of its cognates, appears in each stanza, in the first three as rhyme words, and then in the last line of the poem.

Annotations

Stanza 1

Line 1: this is similar to the opening line of poem 23, 'Perch'i' no spero di tornar giammai'.

Line 2: di sospiri tormento tanto: 'such torment of sighs'. The unusual syntax emphasises sighing as a manifestation of the narrator's pain, but also allows for the alliteration of the last two words.

Line 3: che: this conjunction could either introduce a clause expressing the result of lines 1-2, or be equivalent to the conjunction in line 1.

dell': 'from'.

Line 4: mostrando per lo viso agli occhi morte: 'showing death in my face (**per lo viso**) to the eyes of others (**agli occhi**)'. Nelson has 'Showing death to onlookers' eyes through sight'.

Line 5: sentìo: archaic form of the first person singular preterite, *sentii*.

alquanto: 'at all'.

Line 6: poscia ch': 'since'.

Lines 7-8: it is Love personified who speaks here. Love's address to the lover in poem 9 is very similar. The use of **valor** to describe the lady is repeated in line 22 and line 49, not to mention poem 9, line 5.

Line 9: virtù: 'life-force'. The same term used in the plural appears twice in poem 7 in relation to the narrator. In line 30 the form *vertute* is used to describe the lady.

si partìo: third person singular preterite.

Line 10: poi che lassò: 'having (already) left the heart (to fight the battle alone).

Line 11: la qual degli occhi suoi: refers to the lady, 'who by means of her eyes...'

Line 14: ruppe: Nelson has 'put to rout'. Poem 7 makes use of the same verb and the flight of the spirits.

Stanza 2

Line 15: contare: used in poem 2, where there are many similarities with this stanza.

Line 17: di qua giù: Cavalcanti makes a distinction between the earthly and the heavenly. A similar division is made in poem 2, 'non fu sì alta già la mente nostra'.

Line 18: 'in order that she may be contemplated by our intellect'. To be so contemplated by the intellect, an object must first be held in the mind. This cannot be done in the case of the narrator's lady, as the following lines describe.

Line 19: gentil: 'noble'. See poem 1, line 2. Repeated again in line 30.

Line 21: sì come quella che: really a periphrasis for 'since'.

Line 22: ch'è i llei dimostro: (before the power) 'that is manifest in her'. The line is a periphrasis for 'before her power'.

Line 23: Per gli occhi: 'through my eyes'.

claritate: 'light'. See poem 2, line 2.

Line 24: quale: 'whoever'. The same impersonal commentator is used in poem 8.

Line 25-6: literally the narrator, who has been reduced to death, (**persona morta**) has taken the form of pity (**questa pietate**) in order to ask for mercy (**dimandar merzede**). Nelson's translation maintains the original construction, 'Don't you see this object of pity That is put in place of a dead person To ask for mercy?'

Line 28: E: 'Yet'. Despite the extremity of the lover's situation, the lady has not realised his suffering, or heard his request for mercy.

Stanza 3

Line 31: salute: as in poem 2, line 13, the meaning is closer to 'perfection', or 'ability' than it is to 'physical health'.

Line 32: this line is a variation on lines 17-18.

ardisco: not so much 'dare' (Nelson) as 'be able to'.

star nel pensero: 'persist in the thought' (Nelson).

Line 33: le bellezze sue: are those of the lady. Similarly in poem 9, line 5, Love is a witness to the lady's qualities. Such is the power of this particular lady, however, that even Love is affected in line 39.

Line 34: sbigottisce: see the introduction to Part 3.

Line 36: the speaker is Love.

ti dispero: 'I despair of you, I see no hope for you'.

Line 37: però che: 'since'.

trasse del su' dolce riso / una saetta aguta: 'she shot from her sweet smile a sharp arrow'. It is typical of Cavalcanti to make the woman the subject of such a violent action.

Line 39: 'l tuo core e 'l mio diviso: Love participates in the lover's suffering.

Line 40: quando venisti: 'when you came'. This may refer to the meeting with and speech made by Love in lines 5-8. Contini, however, suggests that it refers to the meeting between the lover and Love which took place in poem 9, where Love says ostensibly the same thing. This is possible, but it does assume a chronology for which there is no definite evidence. It also suggests that Cavalcanti may have thought about his poems in terms of a progression along the lines of *Vita Nuova*, but again there is no evidence that this was ever the case.

Stanza 4

The final stanza is a *congedo* addressed to the canzone itself.

Line 43: libri d'Amore: Cavalcanti is probably not referring to any specific books. He may be referring to the tradition of lyric poetry in general, but it is more likely that the books are a metaphor for the experinece of love in general. In this sense, as De Robertis points out, the trope anticipates Dante's famous manifesto in Purgatorio XXIV, lines 52-54: "'I' mi son un che, quando / Amor mi spira, noto, e a quel modo / ch'e' ditta dentro vo significando'." ['I am one who, when Love breathes / in me, takes note; what he, within, dictates / I, in that way, without, would speak and shape'.].

Line 44: asemplai: 'copy'. Cavalcanti has faithfully copied the model. The implication is that he has made the canzone a true and accurate account of love. The same verb appears in conjuction with the metaphor of the book in the opening lines of the *Vita Nuova*: 'In quella parte del libro de la mia memoria dinanzi a la quale poco si potrebbe leggere si trova una rubrica la quale dice: *Incipit vita nova*. Sotto la quale rubrica io trovo scritte le parole le quali è mio intendimento d'assemplare in questo libello e se non tutte, almeno loro sentenzia'. [In my book of memory, in the early part where there is little to be read, there comes a chapter with the rubric: *Incipit vita nova*. It is my intention to copy into this little book the words I find written under that heading – if not all of them, at least the essence of their meaning.].

Line 45: ti piaccia: '(I hope) you permit, allow (that I put my trust in you)'.

Line 46: e vadi: 'and (I hope) you will go'.

Line 49: soverchio: 'excess'.

Line 50: eran: 'would have been'. The spirits would have been destroyed, if they had not fled (**vòlti**).

Line 51: vanno soli, senza compagnia: echoed in *Inferno* XXIII, line 1, 'Taciti, soli, sanza compagnia / n'andavam ...' [Silent, alone, no one escorting us, / we made our way ...] (Contini).

Line 53: Però li mena per fidata via: 'Therefore lead them by a safe road'.

Line 55: sono in figura: 'represent' or 'are an image of'. See also poem 14, line 8, and poem 20, line 22.

11 *POI CHE DI DOGLIA COR CONVEN CH'I' PORTI*

The theme of this single stanza is the narrator's attempt to demonstrate his predicament. The end of the opening *piede* states the narrator's intention to speak, 'dirò'. This is echoed in line 5, 'E dico'. But the effort at description fails in the *sirima* because the narrator has been overcome by 'lo folle tempo'. He cannot find words or self-assurance to speak, 'sì ch'io non mostro quant'io sento affanno'. The beginning of the poem knows nothing of the failure in the *sirima*, thereby heightening the drama. We do not have 'I would tell ...' from the start, but rather 'I will tell' and then 'I tell you that ...', followed by the admission of failure in the *sirima*.

In the process of describing what it is he cannot describe, the narrator makes use of the characteristic tropes of part 3. Individual lines in the *fronte* are structured around the device of antithesis, and sometimes reveal strong parallels between lines. Lines 2 and 3 offer excellent examples, 'e senta di **piacere** ardente **foco** / e di **virtù** mi traggi' a sì **vil loco**'. The corresponding middle two lines of the second *piede* share a similar symmetrical construction based on antithesis. But, while antithesis dominates as a rhetorical device in the *fronte*, it becomes an explicit thematic force in the *sirima* as the narrator describes the madness which estranges himself from himself, 'mi cangio di mia ferma oppinïone / in altrui condizione'.

There is no version by Rossetti, and one by Pound (1912).

STRUCTURAL NOTE

This poem is a stanza of 15 lines. It is therefore often refered to as a single stanza canzone, though, of course, the sonnet was also originally a single stanza canzone. According to a reading given by Tanturli (1984), and subsequently supported by De Robertis, this canzone undermines its own development before it can proceed beyond the first stanza. In accordance with the genre, the *fronte* sets out the themes to be discussed. But, unusually, the *sirima* contradicts such an aim, citing the narrator's internal instability as a reason for incapacity to demonstrate, 'mostrare', his situation. The poem therefore comes to an abrupt conclusion, as if it were, to paraphrase De Robertis, a modern version of the classical *recusatio*, a poem in which the poet declines to write the poem that he or she set out to write (De Robertis).

As a single stanza the present piece is not unique. Cavalcanti himself wrote one other single stanza poem, 'Se m'ha del tutto oblïato Merzede', and Dante produced two. It was Dante who, in the *De vulgari eloquentia* [II, vi, 6], cited poem 11 as an example of 'gradus constructionis excellentissimus' along with his own 'Amor che ne la mente mi ragiona', and there is no denying that the poem has a formal balance appropriate to its theme. The *fronte* is composed of two *piedi*, ABBC. These are followed by a *sirima* of seven lines, DEeFfGG, where the ninth line is not connected by rhyme to any other, perhaps so that the structure itself could mimick the 'folle tempo' of the narrator's psyche.

ANNOTATIONS

Line 1: literally 'since that of pain the heart it is necessary that I carry', or, arranged for grammatical sense, 'Since it is necessary that I have a suffering heart'. Pound has 'Sith need hath bound my heart in bands of grief'.

Line 2: di: 'in the place of'. The line might therefore read, 'and feel in place of delight, burning fire'. Both Pound and Nelson are incorrect in thinking that the proximity of **piacere** and **ardente foco** must necessarily imply some sort of synonymy, and a reference to physical/sexual pleasure. This is not the case at all. The construction mirrors that of line 1 by employing antithesis. Pound has 'Sith I turn flame in pleasure's lapping fire', and he reinforces this reading with 'I lost a treasure by desire' in the subsequent line. Nelson's 'And feel the burning fire of pleasure' is no better.

piacere: usually translated as 'delight' or 'pleasure', the term is not to be limited, here, to sensual gratification. Indeed in this case it is antithetical to '*ardente foco*'. From the Provençal verb *plazer*, to please, it takes on various meanings in Cavalcanti, of which the most common is 'beauty' as in 'Fresca rosa novella', line 2: 'piacente primavera'. It also has such a meaning in Dante. Foster and Boyde write: '*piacere* frequently has this objective sense of beauty, that which causes joy' (Foster and Boyde 62).

Line 3: again the word order is contorted, possibly in order to have the repeated '*di*' in the first hemistich of verses 1-3. A literal reading might be 'and from virtue I move to such a low place (or state)', though of course **mi traggi** is a stronger verb than 'move'. 'I drag myself against my will, or better intentions', comes closer. Like the two verbs before it, **traggi** is in the subjunctive tense because it is dependent on 'conven'. Here it is reflexive. 'I move from virtue to this low place'.

virtù: certainly intended to link with 'valore' in line 4, and 'possanza' in line 15, and in opposition to 'vil loco'. Again it is a word with a wide range of meanings. As was once also the case with the English equivalent, 'virtue', the word is closer to 'strength' or 'vitality' in Cavalcanti than to any moral goodness, after the Latin *virtus*: 'strength', 'courage'. We find a similar dichotomy in poem 13, line 18, where Love makes the heart's 'virtù in vizio cadere'. Here, too, the poles of difference in the heart are 'strength' and 'weakness', rather than 'virtue' and 'vice'. Pound runs with what he imagines is a moral dimension to the quatrain, though it is quite uncharacteristic of Cavalcanti, 'Sith I turn flame in pleasure's lapping fire, / I sing how I lost a treasure by desire / And left all virtue and am low descended' (lines 2-4).

Line 4: valore: see the discussion of this term in poem 8.

Lines 5-8: the second *piede* of the *fronte* with its opening note of declamation goes part of the way to explicating the narrator's state of being in love, making use of some of the terms which have come to be familiar in the poetry of *sbigottimento*: the death of the spirits, the battle of the heart, the go-between Love made to weep in pity.

Line 5: miei spiriti: 'life forces', or 'vital energy'.

Line 6: che: is not a relative pronoun here, but a conjunction introducing a declarative clause referring to the heart. A literal version might run, 'and that the heart has much of war and little of life'.

Line 7: gioco: 'joy', not 'game' as in current usage. See also poem 2. Literally 'and if it were not that death is a pleasure for me'.

Line 8: fare' ne di pietà pianger Amore: the lover desires death above all else (line 7) because it is seen as the only possible end to his current suffering. In desiring his own destruction the narrator demonstrates the level of irrationality to which he is pushed by Love. In dwelling on death he has some respite, and in death itself relief. If this were not the case (and see poem 22, lines 14-16, where the narrator increases his anxiety by imagining that death will not bring relief), then he could easily make Love weep in pity for his hopeless state of being.

Lines 9-15: the *sirima* opens on an abrupt **Ma** which undermines the declarative tone of the *fronte*. The narrator professes an inability to show, *mostrare*, suggesting that he no longer knows himself and cannot trust himself to speak, before the closing couplet, functioning as a coda, returns to summarise the initial theme.

Line 9: folle tempo: 'madness'.

Line 10: mia ferma opinione: I follow Tanturli's interpretation in reading 'my self understanding, my identity' (Tanturli 16). Pound's translation is more literal, but consequently opaque: 'The firm opinion which I held of late / Stands in a changéd state'. Nelson is better, 'I change from my own set state of mind'.

Line 11: in altrui condizione: 'into a state where I am foreign to myself'.

Line 12: non mostro: 'I am not able to demonstrate' or, rather, 'to describe', since the demonstration is here by way of words.

Line 13: là 'nd': 'for which reason', or 'and so'; not 'there where' as in Pound.

ricevo inganno: 'I am deceived, disillusioned, due to the inability to recount the situation, and the self alienation'. Contini, however, translates 'rimango danneggiato', 'I am injured', citing similar examples in *Inf.* XX 1.96 and *Par.* IX ll.2-3.

Line 14: Amanza: provençialism for *Amore*, used no doubt to facilitate the rhyme with line 15.

Line 15: porta: the repetition of the verb in line 1 suggests that this coda is a summary of the initial theme. Pound was following an erroneous edition which had 'speranza' in place of 'possanza', leading to 'And in her passage all mine hopes were spent'.

12 *PERCHÉ NON FUORO A ME GLI OCCHI DISPENTI*

This poem has strong thematic links with sonnets 8 and 9. Here the narrator has taken a further step into despair: no longer is the point of comparison he who is most happy, 'quei che più allegrezza sente' (poem 8), but rather he who feels great suffering, 'gran pena sente'; just as it is no longer the narrator who calls the reader to make the comparison, but rather an unidentified voice whose post-mortem description of the lover adopts the terms of martyrdom.

The sonnet opens with a resounding note of regret which immediately evokes *Job* III, 10-11: '... quia non conclusit ostia ventris qui portavit me, nec abstulit mala ab oculis meis. Quare non in vulva mortuus sum, egressus ex utero non statim perii?' ['because it shut not up the doors of my mother's womb, nor hid sorrow from mine eyes. Why died I not from the womb? why did I not give up the ghost when I came out of the belly?'] (King James). Pound's translation successfully imitates *Job* here: 'Ah why! why were mine eyes not quenched for me'. The repeated acoustic motif which dominates the first hemistich in lines 1 and 3 ('**non** fuoro a **me**' and '**non** fosse nella **me**nte mia') gives emphasis to the narrator's wish to negate his current situation. At the same time, however, the second hemistiches of these two verses, as well as the second hemistich of line 2, all conclude with the tenth syllable and rhyme on a past participle, bringing home the fact that the narrator dwells on what is unchangeably past.

Once again the narrator describes the process by which the beloved image enters through the eyes and moves into the mind of the lover. According to contemporary systems of physiology, an external impression, gained almost always by the sense of sight, moved first to the individual's *sensus communis*, located at the front of the brain, where it was apprehended and constructed into an image. From there, the image moved to the faculty of estimation, *aestimativa*, in the centre of the brain, where a decision was made as to how to respond to the external object (Boyde 1993 47-48). In the present sonnet the image of the lady is so powerful that the lover's mind has no control over it, and is defeated like a city by an invading army.

Cassata offers some interesting variant readings of the manuscripts. The sonnet is relatively well represented in the extant codices, but there are discrepancies between all of them leading to irresolvable questions of interpretation. First amongst these is the question of whether the soul's direct speech at the end of the octet continues through to the end of the poem, or finishes at the end of line 8. This is an important question because it may alter whether the lady is addressed directly by the narrator or only by the narrator's soul. This has led to speculation that the 'fosse' of line 3 could be 'fossi', therefore indicating a more consistent direct address to the lady throughout the poem. Secondly there is the question of whether or not the 'morto' of line 14 is death personified or an adjective referring to the narrator. Translations exist by Rossetti (XVII Sonnet: Of his Pain from a new Love), and Pound (1912).

STRUCTURAL NOTE

The sonnet has a metrical scheme frequent in Cavalcanti: ABBA ABBA CDE CDE.

ANNOTATIONS

Line 1: fuoro: 'furono', 'were'.

dispenti: 'blinded', although *spegnere* is more literally 'to turn off', or 'extinguish'. Pound adopts 'quenched'; Nelson, 'extinguished'; Rossetti is more liberal with the line, 'Why from the danger did mine eyes not start, / Why not become even blind'.

Line 2: de: 'by means of'.

veduta: 'faculty of sight'.

Line 3: fosse: all existing manuscripts print *fosse*. This is the reading favoured by De Robertis, but it has been questioned by Cassata who prints *fossi*. While the subject is not named, it is (being feminine in the past participle 'venuta') almost certainly the lady who is referred to. Is she addressed directly in the octet of the poem, in which case it would be *fossi* ('you had'), or is the poem addressed to a third party, in which case it would be *fosse* ('she had')? The question is important because one must also establish who it is that speaks throughout the sestet, addressing the lady with the familiar *tu*. Is it the narrator, or does the soul's speech continue from lines 7 and 8? Rossetti adopted *fossi*. Nelson and Pound, however, use *fosse*.

Line 4: ascolta se: literally 'listen if'. But the voice sounds ironic, condescending and very sure of itself.

Lines 5-8: If the opening quatrain may be described as an outburst of regret, the second tells us why the lady's entry into the narrator's mind was so damaging. Most editors consider the soul's speech to continue throughout the sestet as a sort of sermon. It should be considered, however, that some significant factors stand against such a reading. Firstly the sestet opens by shifting the temporal and mental perspective to one of hopelessness, in line with the first quatrain, but different from the plea by the soul in lines 7 and 8. No longer is there a plea for pity in the present, '*ci aiuta*', but rather a switch to the past, '*tu gli ha' lasciati sì*', and a suggestion, in the description by the mysterious voice, that it is too late, that the lover has gone over the brink to death. Secondly if the soul's speech closes at the end of line 8, it results in a structural balance which is not uncommon in Cavalcanti, for in that case direct speech by three different voices closes both quatrains and the sestet. Poem 14 offers a fine example. Pound and Rossetti both follow this argument through, and have the lover, not the soul, speak in the sestet.

Supporting the view that the soul's speech continues throughout the sestet is the fact that the pronoun in line 9 refers to the eyes, which had been introduced in the speech by the soul in line 8.

Line 5: novi tormenti: further suffering as a result of love for the lady.

Line 6: allor: refers back to the period of time in the first *piede* when the lady initially entered the lover's mind.

Line 7: or: 'orsù': interjection. Not, as Nelson has, 'help us now'. Rossetti has 'That, Lady, Lady, (I said,) destroy not quite / Mine eyes and me! Oh help us where thou art!'.

ci aiuta: present imperative with the pronoun placed before the verb.

Line 8: gli occhi ed i': 'the eyes and I (the soul)'. Note the structural balance of the eyes returning to close the octet, just as they opened it. Also of importance is the abrupt caesura after **i'**, which creates an internal rhyme with 'sì' in line 9 (Cassata).

Lines 9-14: there is almost a projection forward in time in the sestet to a moment after the lover's death, as if Love comes, or came, to weep not only out of compassion, but because one of her 'faithful' in love is dead. Or so the voice out of the depths seems to suggest, in whose 'sermon' the lover is held up to all those who suffer as an example, indeed a martyr, for Love.

Line 9: Tu: the lady.

gli ha' lasciati sì: according to De Robertis the adverb emphasises the fact that they were left, rather than referring to how they were left, which has already been conveyed by the use of 'dolenti' in line 8. The object intended is the eyes.

sì, che: a similar construction is found in two other places in the poem: **sì ... che** (lines 6-7), and **tanto che** (line 11). Each time, the construction links one event to the next, creating the impression of a chain reaction, one event arising out of another in quick succession. See poem 16 for another example of this technique.

Line 10: Love comes to weep. Similarly in the previous poem, lines 7-8: 'e se non fosse che 'l morir m'è gioco, / farei' ne di pietà pianger Amore', where Love's compassion is linked to the narrator's desire for death.

Line 11: **profonda voce**: a voice that comes *de profundis*, out of the depths, or, in biblical terms, the *abyssus* (De Robertis). Both Pound and Nelson have 'deep voice'.

Line 12: **chi gran pena sente**: the construction is similar to that in poem 8, line 12, 'Qualunqu'è quei che più allegrezza sente'. The impersonal sufferer is asked to compare him/herself to the lover-martyr of the poem and reflect on the greater suffering of this latter.

Line 13: **vederà 'l su' core**: the heart is that of the lover. This image echoes or is echoed in the famous opening sonnet of the *Vita Nuova*, 'A ciascun alma', and the prose commentary with its 'Vide cor tuum', in which Love holds the narrator's heart in hand.

Line 14: **che Morte**: two readings of this final line are possible, depending on whether **Morte** is taken to be an adjective referring to the lover, or a personification. In the first case one would expect the form of the adjective to have its desinence in 'o' rather than 'e', and in fact some of the important manuscripts in which this poem is found print 'morto'. In such an instance, 'costui' is the subject of the last line and 'che morto' is a subordinate clause, leading to the literal translation: 'this one, who is dead, carries his own heart in his hand'. This is the version favoured by Cassata and given plenty of weight by De Robertis, because it clearly implies the narrator's ostension of his own organ of martyrdom (the heart), just as St Lucia displays her eyes, or St Agatha her breasts. The second possibility is that Death personified carries the lover's heart in his hand, a reading closer to Dante's 'A ciascun alma', though in that instance it was Love who carried the lover's heart. Death is also personified in line 14 of poem 13. In either case the important fact remains that the narrator is associating himself with a death which will stand as an example. He is concerned not only with the attempt to represent his own life, but also with how it will be represented after death and through the act of death itself. There is a clear link to poem 11, where the lover is compared to a statue which 'porti ne lo core una ferita / che sia, com' egli è morto, aperto segno'. Pound is representative of all the other English versions when he writes 'Death beareth in his hand cut cruciform'.

tagliato in croce: unmistakably a reference to the crucifix, and therefore supporting the motif of martyrdom.

13 *QUANDO DI MORTE MI CONVEN TRAR VITA*

This ballad has been described as a poem of oppositions, not only for the frequency of the rhetorical device of antithesis, but for the constant opposition between life and death, love and death, and the ability for things to be other than they appear (De Robertis). Together with poem 22, this poem is an excellent example of how Cavalcanti was able to push the thematic boundaries of the ballad form to include poetic works of great dramatic power and pathos.

There is no version by Rossetti, and one by Pound (1912). There is also a verse translation which follows the rhyme scheme of the original by Hubert Creekmore (Lind 104).

STRUCTURAL NOTE

This ballad consists of a refrain and three stanzas. It is a so-called '*mezzana*', or medium, ballad because the refrain is made up of two hendecasyllables and two *settenari*. In the refrain the rhyme scheme is XyyX. Each stanza is divided into two *mutazioni* and a *volta*. Here the *mutazioni* take the scheme AbC, while the *volta* follows CddX. The refrain sets out the theme, and the stanzas develop and act as variations on that theme. The word *morte*, which appears in the first line is a key. It is repeated once in each stanza.

ANNOTATIONS

Line 1: the antithesis of life and death is representative of the rhetorical device which dominates the entire poem and gives it much of its dramatic power.

Quando: 'since', or 'if'.

di morte mi conven trar vita: Nelson is good: 'Since from death I must draw life'. Pound has altered the spirit of the original, 'If all my life be but some deathly moving, / -Joy dragged from heaviness -'.

trar: the same verb is found in poem 11, line 3. It is also found in line 27.

Line 2: e di pesanza gioia: a common antithesis. The syntactical construction mirrors that of the first line, albeit in a more reductive form, which gives emphasis to the antithesis. The sense is 'and [if I draw all my] joy from pain'.

pesanza: 'pain' or 'suffering'. This is not the only Provençialism in the poem. Apart from its repetition at line 25, one finds 'beninanza' at line 11, and 'amanza' in line 28. While all translators agree on 'joy', their ideas about its linguistic opposite vary dramatically: Pound uses 'heaviness'; Creekmore adopts 'despair'; and Nelson, 'affliction'.

Line 3: come: 'how is it possible that'.

di: 'how is it possible that the spirit of love can draw out from such a state of pain an invitation to love' (see Contini for an alternative interpretation, however). Nelson's translation is most semantically accurate at this point: 'How is it that from such distress / Love's spirit exhorts me to love?'.

tanta noia: synonymous with 'pesanza' in line 2.

Line 4: d'amar: 'ad amare': 'to love'.

Lines 5-14: the first stanza opens by repeating the terms and construction of lines 3 and 4 of the refrain. Indeed the *fronte* is, like the refrain, a single rhetorical question, a variation on, rather than a development of, the theme presented in the first four lines.

Line 5: the spirit of love which allured the narrator is now referred to as the narrator's own heart. The contradiction and antithesis which drove the refrain is seen to exist within the narrator himself. Pound interprets differently. He has the spirit of love inviting the heart: 'How summon up my heart for dalliance?'. Nelson is clearer, 'How is it that my heart exhorts me to love'.

Line 6: lasso: a common interjection expressing dismay. The subject of the line is still the heart.

Line 7: 'and overcome by sighs in every part'.

Line 8: che quasi sol: 'not even'. The line might read therefore 'that he can't even cry for mercy'. Pound has 'that e'en the will for grace dare not advance'.

Line 9: e di vertù lo spoglia: the heart is stripped of virtue by the 'afanno' of the next line. The construction echoes that of lines 2 and 3.

Line 10: già quasi: 'already almost entirely'.

Line 13: guardi ... e miri: the recourse to the impersonal 'everyone' or 'anyone' to testify as to the verity of the lover's predicament is common to many poems. See poems 8, 9, and 12. Pound's embellishment, 'till all men's careless eyes', is out of place.

Line 14: Morte: the first of many appearances of Death personified in this ballad. While life and death were both present in the opening line of the poem, the first stanza opens with a line containing the word 'life', 'inVITA', and closes here with a line containing its opposite.

Lines 15-24: the grammatical subject of the first stanza was the heart. The opening word of the second stanza announces that now it is Love. The *fronte* introduces a familiar description of the process by which Love enters the lover only to 'fa la sua virtù in vizio cadere'. The *sirima* then returns to a rhetorical question which is a variation on that of the refrain. The last three lines then attempt to answer the question.

Line 15: di simil piacere: a difficult expression to interpret. It is best understood as 'by like potential', that is, 'Love is born in one when it sees a similar potential to love in the loved object', or perhaps, more simply, 'one is attracted to people who bear some resemblance to oneself'. A similar idea occurs in poem 18, lines 57-58. Existing English translations have pushed the meaning of the line in another direction. Nelson has 'of mutual pleasure'; Pound, 'Love that is born of loving like delight'; and Creekmore, 'For Love, that of a like delight is born'.

Line 16: si posa: the term recurs in 'Donna me prega' in an identical context: 'là dove posa' (line 10) where the meaning is 'comes to have its rightful seat'.

Line 17: formando di disio nova persona: I have followed other English versions in translating this phrase literally 'forming a new figure of desire'. For Cassata the 'new person' is the individual who is physically transformed by love, as one finds in 'Donna me prega', lines 50-51, '*La nova qualità move sospiri / e vòl ch'om miri 'n non formato loco*'. Love, which has entered the heart, forms or conjures a figure or personification (the **nova persona**) of desire. The term 'desire' should be understood in a generic sense of attraction. This image is mirrored in an identical position in the final stanza, where Death, too, evokes a personification.

Line 18: ma fa la sua virtù in vizio cadere: literally 'but makes his virtue fall into vice'. Various difficulties of interpretation exist here, stemming from whether the subject is *Amore* or 'qual' of line 20; and whether the possessive adjective refers to the heart or, again, *Amore*. English translators have read Love as the subject of the line, but left the possessive adjective ambiguous in some cases. Pound has 'Yet toppleth down to vileness all his [?] might'; Nelson, 'But it makes [heart's] strength decay to weakness'; and Creekmore, 'But tumbles down his [?] might in vicious scorn'. I tend to favour Nelson's reading. Interestingly in order to avoid ambiguity Nelson places the square brackets in his own text (all the other instances are my own). Nelson has also interpreted **virtù** and **vizio** in terms which suit both the immediate context and the physical degeneracy which results from love.

Line 19: già: the adverb reinforces the negative construction. The subject is 'qual' of the next line.

Line 20: qual: the impersonal 'whoever'.

servir: 'offer service to Love'.

guiderdona: 'guerdon', or 'reward'. Love is the subject. Literally: 'whoever feels how Love rewards service done for him'.

Line 21: Love remains the subject.

Line 22-24: Love personified allures the narrator into love because Love sees that the narrator asks assistance of Death in order to escape his suffering. Two possible reasons for Love's action come to mind. Either the narrator wants to escape from Love by embracing Death, and Love is trying to talk him out of it; or, secondly Love is allied with Death and encourages the narrator to love because the consequence of loving is to bring on death. Either way the emphasis of the construction is, once again, on the oxymoronic nature of love.

Line 23: domando mercede [a Morte]: to ask mercy of someone in this context is to put oneself in their power, to become their servant (De Robertis).

Line 24: ch'a ciascun dolor m'adita: Nelson's version is good, 'Of Death, who makes me target of every woe'. Pound has 'While Death doth point me on toward all mischance'; Creekmore, 'While to me every sorrow Death displays'.

Lines 25-34: the final stanza might again be considered a variation rather than a development. If the first stanza introduced the heart as the central character of the poem, and the second showed how the heart was acted upon by Love, then this final stanza sees the heart suffer at the hands of Death.

Line 25: blasmar: 'lament'.

pesanza: 'suffering'.

Line 27: ché Morte d'entro 'l cor me tragge un core: just as in line 17 *disio* was given form in the heart by Love, a similar concept returns in the third line of the last stanza. Death now draws out of the heart another heart (as if the lover's heart had a split personality) which speaks of 'crudele amanza'.

Lines 29-30: this personified heart which speaks of cruel loving torments the narrator, adding to his troubles, in the very place where all his vital energy derives from.

Line 31: **Quel punto maladetto sia**: the point in time is that first moment of loving.

Line 33: **la mia vita fera**: 'my harsh or cruel life'.

Line 34: **li fue, di tal piacere, a lui gradita**: the construction depends on the previous two lines: 'Love was born in such a way that (**in tal manera / che**) the cruelty of my life was for him (**li fue**), pleasingly (**di tal piacere**), gratifying (**a lui gradita**)'. The repetition of the pronouns **li** and **a lui** is pleonastic. So, it seems, is **di tal piacere**, though the noun picks up, and ironically inverts, 'piacere' of line 15.

14 *IO TEMO CHE LA MIA DISAVENTURA*

The word *disaventura* in the opening line is found in two other ballads by Cavalcanti, poem 22 and 'La forte e nova mia disaventura'. On the basis of this word the three poems were grouped together by Favati. This suggests that the misfortune in question refers to a specific incident in the biography of the poet-narrator. It seems more likely, however, that *disaventura* is simply a synonym for the narrator's general state of suffering. The sonnet continues the theme of the narrator's psycho-physical fragmentation at the hands of Love and his lady, and therefore it fits well with part 3. Poem 14 might be called the sonnet of voices. There are four separate voices given direct speech, all of them introduced by the verb *dire*: firstly the I influenced by misfortune, who speaks in line 2; then a thought rising from the heart, which speaks for most of the second quatrain; thirdly a sigh rising from the heart, which speaks in line 11; and finally in the last line an indefinite person the narrator goes in search of, and from whom he would like to be told the contrary to the comand just given by the sigh. Each voice offers conflicting advice, and each arises from the narrator himself, underlying his schizoid nature, and casting a series of by now common topoi in a particularly dramatic light.

Pound has two versions, one unpublished, dated 1910, and the version with changes published in 1912 (from which quotations are taken). There is no version by Rossetti.

STRUCTURAL NOTE
This sonnet has the rhyme scheme ABBA ABBA CDE DCE. In each quatrain and each tercet there is one case of direct speech.

ANNOTATIONS
Line 1: **disaventura**: 'misfortune'. See also poem 22, line 11. Pound uses the noun 'unfortune'. **Disaventura** is linked acoustically to the last word in the next line, **dispero**, thereby underlining the connection between the two concepts for the lover. The same word, **disaventura**, appears in the opening line of a sonnet by Guinizzelli, 'Lamentomi di mia disaventura'. But, whereas the earlier Guido moves from the opening complaint to reaffirm his commitment to Love and the need for patience, Cavalcanti entertains little hope of returning from the brink of death.

Line 2: 'leads me to say, 'I despair'.' As is often the case, Pound aims at something more startling, 'I fear me lest unfortune's counter thrust / Pierce through my throat and rip out my despair' (1912). In the 1910 version this second line had been 'Drive me to publish my bleak despair'.

Line 3: **però ch'**: 'since'.

pensero: the distance of the lover from a rational resonse to his situation is emphasised by that fact that this 'thought' is introduced by the verb *sentire*, speaks of fear, and arises from the heart.

Line 6: **in guisa, che**: 'that'.

di leggero: 'easily'.

Line 7: **contar il vero**: 'express or manifest yourself and your emotional state'.

Line 8: 'without taking on the figure of Death'. Death is once again seen as the extreme of suffering. Nelson has 'without Death transforming you into its likeness'. Pound, 'For fear Death set thee in his reckoning'.

che ... non: 'without'.

Line 9: De: 'As a result of'.

Line 10: uno sospiro: even the lover's sigh is personified and given voice.

Line 11: spiriti: these, and the **Spiritei** of line 14 (a diminutive form), are the vital spirits, or life force.

Line 12: miro: 'seek'. 'Then I seek out a compassionate man' (Nelson). The **uom** is similar to the indefinite figure who corroborates the lover's suffering from an objective viewpoint in poem 8. Here the lover, who has lost all volition, requires the impersonal voice not only to comment on his situation but to actively console and counsel him. The version used by Pound read 'null'uom', leading to: 'And of all piteous folk I come on none / Who seeing me so in my grief's control / Will aid by saying e'en: 'Nay, Spirits, wait!''.

PART FOUR: IN PRAISE OF LOVE

15 – *Un amoroso sguardo spiritale*
16 – *Veggio negli occhi de la donna mia*
17 – *Pegli occhi fere un spirito sottile*

Cavalcanti is best known for the canzone 'Donna me prega' and the compositions in part 3 recounting the destructive nature of love. A few important poems in praise of love and the narrator's lady have also survived, poems which cannot simply be grouped with those early compositions in part 1.

These praise poems differ from the earlier poems for a range of reasons. 'Un amoroso sguardo spiritale' combines elements of praise with elements closer to the poems of *sbigottimento*. 'Veggio negli occhi de la donna mia', by contrast, describes the miraculous apparition of the lady in terms which extend the treatment found in poem 2. Both poems 15 and 16, however, are new because whether they are describing the lady, or love, they do so in terms which take their bearings from the narrator's own experiences and sentiments. Even 'Veggio negli occhi della donna mia' is firmly grounded in the framework of the narrator's own sensations, as the opening verb reveals. By contrast, such an egocentric investigation of love is absent from poems 1 and 2.

Poem 17, 'Pegli occhi fere un spirito sottile', is somewhat different. The description of love is optimistic, but focus on the lover-narrator of other poems has disappeared. The discussion of love is impersonal. Cavalcanti reminds readers of his presence not as the I of the poem but through the playfulness of spirit and technical bravura which sees the word *spirito* or its cognate *spiritello* in each line.

The significance of the praise style developed in these later pieces cannot be underestimated. Especially in the case of 'Veggio negli occhi de la donna mia', the experience Cavalcanti set down was of fundamental importance in the development of Dante's lyric poetry, and particularly in his discovery of a new language for the praise poem (De Robertis 85). Despite being few in number, the poems in part 4 play an important role in the legacy Cavalcanti left to the emerging lyric tradition.

15 *UN AMOROSO SGUARDO SPIRITALE*

This delightful sonnet finds a balance between the positive, salvific aspects of the woman's power over the lover, and the negative, destructive aspects that dominated part 3. The sweetness of love is embodied by the 'amoroso sguardo spiritale' in line 1, which returns to open the sestet, 'sì dolce sguardo'. This is the dominant theme of the poem. Love is now a vital force that renews and infuses the lover with a spirit of joy. At the same time such enthusiasm is balanced by the second quatrain, where the lady abandons the lover to his suffering. And just as the sweet *sguardo* that brings life returns in the first tercet, so the theme of pity returns in the second tercet. Once again the impetus for celebration has turned out to be a plea for more attention.

Guinizzelli offers an interesting point of comparison. In his canzone 'Madonna, il fino amore ch'io vi porto' one finds the following:

> *Sottil voglia vi poteria mostrare*
> *Come di voi m'à priso amore amaro,*
> *ma ciò dire non voglio,*
> *ché 'n tutte guise vi deggio laudare;*
> *per ch'e' più dispietosa vo'n dechiaro*
> *se blasmo vo ' nde toglio.* [Lines 25-30]

> [A crafty mind might be able to show you
> how bitter love has conquered me for you;
> but I don't want to say that,
> for I must praise you in every way;
> and so I declare you even more pitiless
> if I absolve you of blame in this.]

Guinizzelli's threat to complain about the bitterness of love, *amore amaro*, is quickly withdrawn. Cavalcanti, on the other hand, openly indulged in such descriptions for his poems of *sbigottimento*. Here a dramatic tension arises from the juxtaposition of the two conflicting sentiments evoked in the narrator-lover.

There is one by Pound (1912), but none by Rossetti.

STRUCTURAL NOTE

The poem's rhyme scheme is ABAB ABAB CDE CDE. The frequency of enjambement is noteworthy, particularly in the quatrains. This sonnet is also remarkable for the elegant balance of the two opposing thematic strains mentioned above, to each of which is dedicated a quatrain and a tercet.

ANNOTATIONS

Line 1: **spiritale**: not 'spiritual' but rather, 'in the form of a spirit'. The original construction allows the personified *sguardo* to be the principal actor in the quatrain. This is strengthened by the return of the 'gaze' as the principal grammatical subject in line 9. Nelson maintains the abstraction of the original with 'spirit-glance', but he alters the focus of the *incipit* by placing the subject, Love, up front: 'Love has again aroused in me a loving / spirit-glance'. Nelson's version also seems to suggest that the spirit-glance has come from within the narrator, and not, as the original makes evident, from the lady. Pound has 'A love-lit glance with living powers fraught'.

Lines 1-4: the *sguardo spiritale* is the focus of the quatrain, and it is not until the opening of the second quatrain that the lady is introduced; by assumption, the reader is led to associate the *sguardo* with her. In this way, however, a distinction remains between the positive effect of the personified *sguardo*, and the negative associations the lady produces in the narrator. The lady starts the narrator thinking about how little sympathy she offers him.

Line 2: **m'ha rinovato Amor**: Love is personified here. I have followed Cassata over De Robertis in indicating the personification with a capital letter. I have altered the original slightly, however, in making 'the gaze' the subject (as it is in line 9), and Love an assistant.

Line 3: assa' più che non sòl: 'that much more than was usual'.

m'assale: Nelson and Pound both have 'assails me'.

Line 4: stringem': 'compels me'.

coralemente: 'with the heart', or 'wholeheartedly'. Pound has 'And cordially he driveth me in thought', where the adverb refers not to the narrator's thinking, but rather to Love's driving.

Lines 5-8: the second quatrain marks a decided change in tone. If the first was characterised by the rhyme words 'piacente' and 'coralemente', the second, by contrast, contains the rhymes 'sofferente' and 'poca... vita sente'.

Line 5: verso cu' non vale: 'for whom [my suffering, piety, etc] have no weight'.

Line 6: merzede, ... pietà ... star soffrente: the first two, 'mercy' and 'pity', are practically synonyms (Branca), and could refer either to the narrator's asking for mercy, or the lady's unwillingness to feel it. Both words return in the final tercet, where their usage is more restricted: the lover asks the lady for mercy, and wishes she could feel some pity. The third term, **star soffrente**, refers to an individual's being in a state of suffering. Nelson has 'to whom neither favor / Nor pity nor forbearance has any effect'; while Pound writes 'vaileth not / Mercy nor pity nor the suffering wrought'.

Line 7: ché: 'since'.

soventora: 'often'.

mi dà pena tale: 'she causes me such suffering'.

Line 8: Nelson has 'That only in small part does my heart feel life'; Pound, 'That my heart scarce can feel his life at all'.

Line 9: sento: note the contrast with the same verb in the previous line.

Line 10: d'entro: 'through'. The image passes through the eyes and comes to rest in the heart, where, in line 11, it imbues the narrator with a spirit of joy.

Line 12: di farne a lei mercé: 'to thank her for it'.

Line 13: 'Would that she were so entreated by Love' (Nelson). The **così** which opens the line is augural (De Robertis), but it also links the phrase to the previous lines: just as he is inspired to ask mercy of the lady, so he hopes she will not be adverse to hearing it.

Line 14: no i fosse noia: 'was not a nuisance to her'. Nelson has 'that a little pity would not annoy her'. Pound has interpreted the last two lines differently: 'Love asked her to do this, and that explaineth / Why this first pity doth no annoy'.

16 *VEGGIO NEGLI OCCHI DELLA DONNA MIA*

This important ballad describes the appearance of the lady and her miraculous ascension into the heavens. In the four line refrain a vision of the loved lady enters the narrator and reawakens his hope of life and love. This beatific sight is that act of mercy which the narrator had been pleading his lady to give him so unsuccessfully in part 3. The two stanzas which follow are unlike anything in the previous lyric tradition. For this reason they have received considerable critical attention, and have come to be seen as the precursors of much in Dante's own praise style.

The first stanza attempts to track the rapid succession of images, impressions and sensations which make up the vision of the lady. The rather complex description may be summarised as follows: from out of the lady's countenance, another, more perfect lady seems to issue. This is a personification of beauty, and it overwhelms the lover. In the moment of overwhelming him, and before he has time to make sense of it, a further lady arises from out of the previous one. She, in turn, is an even more perfect embodiment of beauty. But, before the narrator is able to make sense of her, a star rises from the same source, and pronounces the prophetic words, 'your health has arrived'.

These visions arising out of each other are a way of giving form, in poetry, to what the narrator tells us is inexpressible in language. For this reason a new vision arises from the present one precisely at the moment when this first one overwhelms the narrator's senses. The syntax of the lines contributes to the effect. The frequent enjambements suggest that the descriptions themselves will not fit into the normal parameters of the line.

In the second stanza an unidentified voice speaks in biblical tones and announces that the lady's virtue is rising up to heaven. Interestingly there is a shift in time. The voice is said to come before the narrator experiences the sight of the lady in the first stanza, as if to announce her arrival. But the voice's closing words seem to be a commentary on what is taking place as the narrator experiences the vision. The two stanzas really stand beside each other in time. Even the apparatus of chronological progression has been abandoned.

Marti saw in this ballad a poetic description of the process of moving from sensorial beauty to intellectual beauty, a movement culminating in an abstracting process that takes us to the universal form of beauty and the intellectual knowledge of that form, which is beatitude (Marti 401). Cavalcanti aims to render that abstract beauty in a perceptible form. Accordingly each step of the vision is described as a personification. The entire poem refutes the popular contemporary perception of Cavalcanti described by Boccaccio: 'Guido alcuna volta speculando molto abstratto dagli uomini divenia' [Guido sometimes in his philosophical reflections became very cut off from fellow men] (*Decameron*, VI, 9, 9). On the contrary, as a poet Cavalcanti brings the abstract closer to the human through such techniques as personification.

'Veggio negli occhi de la donna mia' is closely linked to a second ballad (both are found together in the same manuscript tradition and in Favati's ordering), 'Posso degli occhi miei novella dire'. The opening line of the present ballad echoes or is echoed in the *incipit* of the second stanza of 'Posso degli occhi': 'Io veggio che negli occhi suoi risplende' [I see resplendent in her eyes]. In fact, in their respective refrains, both ballads seem to mirror each other. Here is the refrain of 'Posso degli occhi': 'Posso degli occhi miei novella dire, / la qual è tale che piace sì al core / che di dolcezza ne sospir' Amore'. [I can say something new about my eyes / Which is such a thing that so pleases the heart / That Love sighs over it for its sweetness] (trans. Nelson).

Cavalcanti's experiments in the praise poem were to have an important influence on the later tradition. In the development of Dante's own praise style (particularly in 'Tanto gentile, tanto onesta pare') this ballad cannot be underestimated.

There is one by Pound (1912), but no version by Rossetti. A prose translation exists by Goldin.

STRUCTURAL NOTE

The poem is a *ballata grande* composed entirely of hendecasyllables. Two eight line stanzas rhyming ABBA ACCZ follow the four line refrain, XYYZ. The use of enjambement disrupts the traditional divisions into *mutazioni* and *volte*. This is particularly evident in lines 7-12. The form mimics the process of miraculous apparitions born one out of another so quickly that '*la mente / comprender no la può*'. In all, there are seven cases of enjambement in the sixteen lines of the two stanzas.

The structure of the traditional ballad tended towards a circular movement. The refrain returned after each stanza, and was linked to each stanza by the Z rhyme. Here, by contrast, the enjambement contributes to a strong forward impetus. The *volta* is not clearly separated from the first half of the stanza. Furthermore the assonance between 'apparita' in line 12 and 'appare' in line 13 is reminiscent of the *coblas capfinidas*.

ANNOTATIONS

Line 1-2: the opening finds numerous echoes in Dante. These may be detected in the *incipit* of Dante's sonnet 'De gli occhi de la donna mia si move / un lume sì gentil, che dove appare' [From my lady's eyes there comes a light so noble that where it appears]; in his famous canzone 'Donne ch'avete intelletto d'amore', lines 52-53: 'De li occhi suoi, come ch'ella li mova, / escono spiriti d'amore inflammati' [From her eyes, wherever she turns them, come fiery spirits of love]; and, finally, in 'Tanto gentile, tanto onesta pare', 'e par che de la sua labbia si move / un spirito soave pien d'amore / che va dicendo a l'anima "Sospira"' [and from her lips seems to come a spirit, gentle and full of love, that says to the soul: 'Sigh'].

Line 3: porta uno piacer novo: the pleasure is spiritual and mental as much as it is physical. Nelson has 'That brings a fresh pleasure to my heart'; Goldin, 'which bears to the heart a sweetness never known'; and Pound, 'Which bear in strange delight on my heart's care'.

Line 4: d'allegrezza vita: 'a life of happiness'. Nelson maintains the original construction, 'vitality of joy'; while Pound writes 'Till Joy's awakened from that sepulchre'. But both underestimate the importance of the word 'life' in a key position. **Vita**, the last word in the refrain, rhymes with the last word of each stanza, *apparita* and *salita*.

Line 5: Cosa: 'an ineffable something'. Nelson is good here, 'Something happens to me when I am in her presence / That I cannot express to the intellect'. Pound's translation has more syntactic ostentation: 'That which befalls me in my lady's presence / Bars explanations intellectual'.

Line 7: labbia: synecdoche for 'face' or 'countenance'.

Lines 7-8: despite the ineffable nature of the vision, lines 7-12 are concerned with the attempt to describe it. Out of the lady's face steps a personification of beauty (**una sì bella donna**). Nelson has 'I seem to see issuing from her countenance / So beautiful a lady'; Pound, 'I seem to see a lady wonderful / Spring forth between her lips'.

Lines 8-9: once again the sonnet 'Tanto gentile e tanto onesta pare' reveals its affiliation with the present ballad: **la mente / comprender no la può** is remarkably similar to Dante's 'che 'ntender no la può chi no la prova' [such as none can understand but he who experiences it].

Line 10: ne nasce un'altra di bellezza nova: 'yet another lady personifying a more perfect beauty'. The chain of images suggests an unfolding flower bud, or the lover's growing insight into the complexity of the initial image.

Lines 11-12: una stella si mova e dica: the star, too, is personified.

si mova: a variation on **uscire** (line 7) and **nasce** (line 10). Nelson has 'From whom a star seems to come / And say'; Pound, 'From whom a star goes forth and speaketh thus'.

Line 12: La salute tua è apparita: note the echo of St Paul, *Titus*, II, xi: 'Apparuit gratia Dei salvatoris nostri'; and *Psalms* XXXIV, 3, 'Dic animae meae: Salus tua eo sum'; and also that of the, *Vita Nuova*, II, 5, 'Apparuit iam beatitudo vestra'. Each of these passages confirms the perfection and beatitude of the vision (De Robertis). Indeed all previous English translators have adopted the word 'salvation' in place of **salute**.

Line 13: questa bella donna: this is the narrator's original lady of line 1, not one of the apparitions described in the previous stanza.

Line 14: s'ode una voce: the unidentified voice comes before the lady, as if to herald her arrival, and is another biblical topos.

Line 15: d'umiltà il su' nome canti: the voice sings of the lady, giving her the name of humility. This is the interpretation which is also offered by De Robertis, and is similar to the description of the lady in poem 2, lines 7-8, 'cotanto d'umiltà donna mi pare / ch'ogn'altra ver' di lei i' la chiam'ira'. Nelson, however, interprets **d'umiltà** as an adverb pertaining to the verb *cantare*, 'And seems in awe to sing her name / so sweetly'. Pound avoids the question in writing 'And seems to sing her name with such sweet praise'. Goldin is more accurate when he writes 'and it seems, moved by her humility it sings her name'.

Line 16: s'i' 'l vo' contare: the verb, meaning 'to describe', appears, again, in poem 2, suggesting a close link between both these praise poems.

Line 17: 'l su' valor: could be either that of the lady, or of the name which is sung by the voice. Goldin is more literal here: 'so sweetly, that if I try to describe it, / I feel how her worth makes me tremble'.

Line 18-19: there is a parallel with the close of the first stanza, both end with direct speech introduced by the verbs *movere* and *dire* (De Robertis).

sospiri: these personified sighs are closely related to the body's internal spirits.

Lines 19-20: Guarda...: the **coste'** is obviously the narrator's lady. Nelson has '"Look; if you gaze on that one / You will see her essence gone up to heaven"'. Pound maintains the original construction, '"Look well!

For if thou look on her, / Then shalt thou see her virtue risen in heaven"'.

17 *PEGLI OCCHI FERE UN SPIRITO SOTTILE*

This sonnet differs from the previous two poems of praise. While it offers a relatively optimistic depiction of love, it is in fact much closer to 'Donna me prega' for two reasons: firstly in both poems Cavalcanti describes the process of being in love impersonally; secondly both poems are playful in spirit. In the present instance this playfulness derives from the challenge Guido has set himself to use the word *spirito* or one of its cognates in every line. Given his predilection for the word, it is tempting to consider the poem as an expression of self-directed irony. The word appears on fifteen occasions (in line 12 there are two examples). The term 'spirit' is used in a range of ways. In the opening lines it is close to the use made of the word by contemporary natural philosophy. But in line 5 it is a synonym for 'person', and in line 10 the sweet and gentle spirit which arises in the lover is closer to a personification of the feeling of happiness. The spirit of love that appears in line 3 might be considered the main protagonist of the quatrains, while the spirit of mercy of line 11 has a similar role in the sestet. On five occasions the diminutive form *spiritello* is used in place of *spirito*, most probably for the sake of variation and to accommodate the hendecasyllable.

There is no version by Rossetti. Pound published two quite different versions, the first in 1912, the second in 1932. In the 1932 version he uses a range of words to translate *spirito* and its cognates: these include 'breath', 'air', 'spryte', as well as 'spirit'.

STRUCTURAL NOTE
The rhyme scheme for this sonnet is ABBA ABBA CDE CDE. Not only is *spirito* or *spiritello* found in each line, but the position of these words is significant. In every line, except the sixth, *spirito* or *spiritello* has its stress

on the fourth or sixth metrically relevant syllable, so that it is emphasised by the metrical ictus of the line. This symmetry is most notable in the sestet, where all the lines are *a maiore*: lines 9-10 and 13-14 have the word *spirito* with its stress falling on the sixth metrically relevant syllable; lines 11-12 have the word *spiritello* with its principal stress falling on the sixth metrically relevant syllable.

ANNOTATIONS

Line 1: Pegli occhi: 'through the eyes'.

fere: suggests the typical battle imagery of the topos, or even Love's arrow.

spirito sottile: this is the image of the lady. This spirit enters the lover via the eyes and, in line 2, moves to the mind.

Line 2: the spirit awoken in the mind by the image of the lady is perhaps a personification of that first shock or fancy that the lady causes.

Line 3: In turn, a spirit of Love is generated. This spirit is the main protagonist in the process that follows. **Si move:** (repeated in line 9) 'arises'.

Line 4: the spirit of Love ennobles (**fa gentile**) all the lover's vital spirits, **ogn'altro spiritel**. There are various versions of the original in this line. Contini prefers 'ch'ogn'altro spiritel[lo] fa gentile'. Cassata suggests 'e fa ogn'altro spiritel gentile'. In any case, the sense of the line is not in question.

Line 5: spirito vile: in this case 'spirit' is used as a synonym for 'person'. Anyone who is **vile**, the opposite of **gentile** in the previous line, is incapable of feeling or knowing the spirit of Love (**lu'**). Similarly in poem 18, lines 6-7: 'perch'io no spero ch'om di basso core / a tal ragione porti canoscenza'. In the previous line the spirit of love is able to ennoble a lover's vital spirits. It would seem, however, that the **spirito vile** is too lowly to receive Love's ennobling spirit.

Line 6: di cotanta vertù spirito: this spirit and the *spiritel* of the next two lines all refer to the spirit of Love of line 3. **Vertù** is virtue in a general sense, the sum of perfection and nobility, and in opposition to **vile**.

Line 7: fa tremare: see poem 16, line 17, and poem 2, line 2.

Line 8: umìle: 'charitable' or 'benevolent'. Love can also exert an influence on the lady, although this does not happen very frequently in Cavalcanti.

Line 9: questo spirito: the spirit of Love.

Line 10: un altro dolce spirito soave: this new sweet and gentle spirit is a personification of the feeling of happiness. Dante echoes this line in 'Tanto gentile e tanto onesta pare' when he speaks of how the lady 'dà per li occhi una dolcezza al core' [through the eyes she sends a sweetness into the heart]. While Dante's sweetness doesn't take the form of a spirit here, it does so two lines later in lines 12-13, 'si mova / un spirito soave pien d'amore' [a spirit comes, gentle and full of love].

Line 11: che siegue: 'that is followed by'.

un spiritello di mercede: 'a spirit of Mercy'. This could be a personification of the benevolent stance of the lady towards the lover, or a second visible manifestation of the feeling of happiness of the previous line, this time with a hint of mercy and benevolence. Nelson has 'which is followed by a little spirit of favor'. Pound, 'that Mercy's spirit followeth his ways' (1912), and 'causeth to follow after him a spirit of pity' (1932).

Line 12: spiriti piove: the spirit of mercy causes a rain of spirits. Piove is used as a transitive verb. These spiriti are a personification of sighs that arise in the lover. Pound has 'from the which a very rain of spirits poureth out' (1912).

Line 13: 'For it has the key to each spirit' (Nelson). Ciascun spirit' refers to the sum of the lover's vital spirits.

Line 14: per forza d': 'thanks to', 'by virtue of'.

uno spirito che 'l vede: 'a spirit that sees him'. Him refers to the spirit of mercy, which holds sway over all the lover's spirits because it has been seen by a spirit of sight (uno spirito che … vede). This spirit that sees is a circumlocution to say the spirit of mercy is visible and, therefore, that it has taken a material form. Phrased in this way the faculty of sight is given its due importance (opening and closing the sonnet and accompanied in both lines 1 and 14 by the preposition per) as it has in the process of love, and as it had in poem 15. The spirit of Love that was sighted at the beginning is balanced by the spirit of mercy sighted here.

PART FIVE: LOVE DEFINED

18 – *Donna me prega, per ch'eo voglio dire*

In many ways this canzone stands alone in Cavalcanti's corpus, both in its ambitious size and structure, and for its technical vocabulary and scholastic rigour. Like much of the lyric poetry of the *Duecento*, it is concerned with defining the nature of love; and yet there is nothing quite like it, either in Cavalcanti or in other authors of the day. True, it has in common with Guido's other poetry a conception of love as, primarily, a physical experience. But, unlike the poems in part 3, love is not represented through its detrimental effects on the narrator, and, unlike the poems of praise, it is not embodied by a particular lady. Here the narrator discusses love in the abstract, love as an *accidente*, the technical term found in line 2. The differences in this poem are reflected in the changes in language. A range of terms have been adopted from scholastic philosophy. To give an idea of the uniqueness of the poem, it is worth noting that there are no less than sixty words here, including *accidente*, which are not found in any other place in Guido's corpus.

Cavalcanti's capacity in 'Donna me prega' to synthesise a philosophical tradition concerning the nature of love with poetic bravura on a formal level led to the poem's enormous popularity in the centuries immediately following its creation. We know this from the number of surviving manuscripts that contain the canzone. From soon after its composition, it began to attract both fame and critical attention (as it continues to do today). Dino del Garbo, medical doctor and philosopher who died in 1327, produced a commentary on the poem written in Latin. This was followed a century later by another, shorter commentary by Marsilio Ficino, again in Latin.[15]

The fame of this particular poem also played a big part in the image that emerged of Cavalcanti as philospher first and poet second, or even as a poet who had rejected literature in favour of natural philosophy.[16] Boccaccio may have been summarising the popular view of Cavalcanti in the *Decameron*, but he certainly also influenced future perceptions, when he wrote, 'egli fu un de' miglior loici che avesse il mondo e ottimo filosofo naturale' [He was one of the best logicians in the world and an excellent natural philosopher][VI, 9, 8].

Much recent interest has continued to focus on attempts to read the poem as a philosophical text, and ascertain Cavalcanti's position on love and religion, and in particular whether he may have been an Averroist or an atheist. The scholarship in this direction is vast, and I make no attempt to encompass it here.[17] It is vital to remember that 'Donna me prega' is, above all, a poem, dominated by a rare structural complexity, and infused with a playful spirit and irony.

In some editions 'Donna me prega' is preceded by a sonnet addressed to Cavalcanti by Guido Orlandi, 'Onde si move, e donde nasce Amore?' [How does love work and where is it born?]. The sonnet is a series of nine questions pertaining to the nature of love, before the final two lines, 'Io domando voi, Guido, di lui: / odo che molto usate in la sua corte' [I ask you, Guido, of Love: / for I hear you are often in his court]. The sonnet shares four of its five rhyme-endings with the canzone (one for each stanza). In placing Orlandi's sonnet before 'Donna me prega', editors have assumed that Cavalcanti was inspired to write his canzone in response to Orlandi. There is no proof of this, nor is there much consensus. Favati, for example, puts forward the hypothesis that Orlandi's sonnet was written subsequently to 'Donna me prega'.

STRUCTURAL NOTE

The canzone consists of five stanzas, each of fourteen lines, each line a hendecasyllable. The *fronte* of each stanza consists of two *piedi* which rhyme ABC. The *sirima*, in turn, has two *volte* rhyming DEFF. But the metrical pattern is rendered more intricate thanks to a series of internal rhymes. Each *piede* has four internal rhymes, one in both the first and third line, and two in the second, giving the pattern (g)A(h)(h)B(b)C, where the parentheses denote the internal rhymes. In each *volta* there are two internal rhymes, D(d)E(e)FF. Finally there is a *congedo*, or closing refrain, of five lines, which follows the scheme XY(y)X(x)ZZ. As Pound noted, this highly formalized structure sees 52 of the 154 syllables in each stanza bound by rhyme (Anderson 206).

'Donna me prega' also has a careful thematic structure. The first stanza introduces the theme of the canzone as a whole and lists a series of eight questions. These eight questions are then dealt with one by one in the space of the ensuing four stanzas; to each is dedicated either a *fronte* or a *sirima*. The *congedo* then follows.

THE ENGLISH TRANSLATIONS

Pound produced two English versions of this canzone. He did not include a version in his first publication of translations of Cavalcanti, *The Sonnets and Ballate of Guido Cavalcanti* (1912), though its *congedo* appears at the end of the 'Introduction'. Rossetti had left no translation of the poem; indeed, he had criticised the canzone as a dull, scholastic analysis of love, lacking emotion. Pound echoed this opinion in his 1913 essay on Cavalcanti. He first translated 'Donna me prega' for *The Dial* 85 (July 1928), and this version was subsequently published in the volume *Guido Cavalcanti Rime: Edizione rappezzata fra le rovine* (1932). A second version, completely reworked, and without the Italian text, as if to suggest a greater independence from the original, was published in 1934 as part of *Eleven New Cantos*.

Pound arranged his first version in such a way that it is difficult to find a clear metrical pattern. There are rhymes at the ends of lines, and internally, but these lack consistency. Curiously Pound has printed the *fronte* and *sirima* of each original stanza as separate strophes, giving the impression that there are eleven stanzas, rather than five plus the *congedo*. Each stanza strays from the number of lines in the original. In this way Pound's version of 'Donna me prega' differs from his other Cavalcanti translations. This is not in itself a criticism. On the contrary, the requirements of rhyme are virtually impossible to reproduce, and in Pound's use of broken lines and internal rhyme something of the playful spirit of the original has been transmitted.

The second version follows the original structure more closely. There are five fourteen line stanzas followed by refrain. The lines, though of varying length, are not broken up by internal rhyme to the same extent, and often assonance takes the place of rhyme. The result is a version which does not draw attention to itself on a syntactical level, as the more contorted first version does.

There are also versions by Goldin (in prose) and Wilhelm (with rhyme). Wilhelm does not follow the rhyme scheme of line-endings exactly, nor is he consistent from stanza to stanza, but rhyme remains a presence. He has made no attempt to reproduce the internal rhymes.

The scholastic language of the original has led to a greater similarity amongst translations on a lexical level. If we take a passage such as lines 21-28, there are no less than eleven terms of a technical nature: *veduta forma, possibile intelletto, subietto, loco e dimoranza, possanza, qualitate, perpetual effetto, diletto, consideranza,* and *similglianza.* Such expressions have been translated in all versions with an equivalent English term, even where scholars may still be debating the meaning of the term.

ANNOTATIONS

Stanza 1

Line 1: **Donna me prega**: 'A lady asks me'. The identity of the lady is unknown and largely irrelevant, although some scholars have discussed the question at length.[18] The invitation to speak which the lady extends is a convention of the treatise writing tradition, such as one finds in the opening of Cappellano's *De amore* (De Robertis). The opening alerts readers to the scientific nature of the investigation.

per ch'eo voglio dire: the conjunction is consecutive, 'and so I would speak'. Here, also, there is a clear echo of such standard openings as Giacomo da Lentini's 'Madonna, dir vo voglio', and Guittone's 'Voglia de dir giusta ragion m'ha porta'.

Line 2: **d'un accidente**: this term, taken from the vocabulary of natural philosophy, was used to refer to something which doesn't have a material existence and can exist only within something else: a mood or passion, for example. It is best described in opposition to *sustanza*, a material substance, as Dante defines it in *Vita Nuova* XXV, 'Amore non è per sé sì come sustanza, ma è uno accidente in sustanzia' [Love is not in itself like a substance, but is an accident within a substance]. While the majority of English versions adopt 'accident' and include a note to define the term, Pound uses 'affect' in both his versions.

che sovente è fero / ed è sì altero: 'which is often fierce and so strong', being by nature a passion. Savona uses the adjectives *tormentoso* and *crudele* to describe **fero**. It is close in meaning to **altero** in the next line (Contini suggests they are synonyms), though Savona translates 'potente' in this second case. Given the imprecision of such adjectives, the translator is always going to run into trouble, and various English versions testify as much. Nelson has 'that is often unruly / and so haughty'; Goldin, 'cruel' and 'unmerciful'; Wilhelm, 'that often fiercely smarts / And is so high'. Pound chose unusual adjectives in 1928, 'that comes often and is fell / And is so overweening'; while he is more direct in 1934, 'wild often / That is so proud'.

Line 3: ch'è chiamato amore: 'so powerful and cruel is the nature of this passion that it is called love'. It is important that the 'thing' which the poem describes is not named as Love until the end of the first *piede*, and only once we know it is an 'accidente', and 'fero' and 'altero'.

Line 4: sì chi lo nega possa 'l ver sentire: the construction expresses a wish: 'would that he who denies that [the nature of love] were able to feel its truth' (Nelson). Other translators have followed Pound in constructing the phrase differently: 'Who denies it can hear the truth now' (1934).

Line 5: Ed a presente: 'And at this point' or 'To this effect'.

conoscente chero: 'I ask for (I want) a competent audience'. The requirement of an appropriate audience returns in the envoi, 'c'hanno intendimento', and is frequent in Dante's lyric poetry. Whereas, in Dante, the competence required is in questions of love and gentility, here the reader needs to have a detailed understanding of natural philosophy and its modalities of argument, the 'natural dimostramento' of line 8.

Line 6: perch'io no spero: Identical clause in the opening of poem 22.

ch'om di basso core: a person of low or ignoble understanding and sentiments, lacking in the noble spirit which Dante made the prerequisite for an understanding of some of his compositions.

Line 7: Nelson's version of lines 5-7 reads: 'And for the present purpose I want someone nobly knowledgeable / As I do not expect that anyone base-hearted / Could bring knowledge to such an argument'.

Lines 8-9: 'since it is not my intention to attempt to demonstrate … [here the eight questions are presented] without adopting a scientific method'.

natural dimostratmento: a method or demonstration which follows natural philosophy, or the effects of Love on the psycho-physical level of the individual. Nelson translates 'philosophical demonstration'; Pound (1934), 'natural demonstration'; Wilhelm 'natural science'; and Goldin, 'natural philosophy'. Pound's first version leaves out the expression.

Lines 10-14: the last five lines of the opening stanza introduce the eight questions which the poet-scientist will answer in the course of the canzone. The questions correspond not only to the list in Orlandi's sonnet discussed in the introduction, but also, as De Robertis points out, to the opening of book 1 of Cappellano's *De amore*.

1/ là dove posa: 'where it installs itself'. As an *accidente*, it must find a subject in which to dwell.

2/ chi lo fa creare: 'who or what creates or gives birth to it'.

3/ e qual sia sua vertute: its qualities or virtues.

4/ e sua potenza: the effects which Love provokes in whoever loves.

5/ l'essenza poi: what is essential and unique to Love.

6/ e ciascun suo movimento: close to question 4, regarding the potentiality of Love. Nelson is right to suggest 'stir', 'what passions does love stir in the lover'.

7/ e 'l piacimento che 'l fa dire amare: 'the pleasurableness that makes it called Love' (Nelson).

8/ e s'omo per veder lo po' mostrare: 'whether Love be visible to human sight', though the construction is literally 'whether man can represent Love visibly [in his sight]'.

Stanza 2

Line 15-20: Guido answers the first question: **dove posa**.

Line 15: memora: 'memory'. Love comes to reside in the memory, and creates a sensory impression in the sensitive soul of the individual, having entered through the eyes, as we are told in line 21.

Lines 16-17: formato, come / diaffan da lume, d'una scuritate: Just as transparency is given form by light, so Love is given form by a certain darkness. The description takes the form of simultaneous analogy and opposition, the sense being that whatever is transparent by nature – air, water, sky, crystal – has form and existence only as a result of light: air for example is not visible and has no form at night. Love, in opposition, is given its form by a certain darkness, as described in line 18. Nelson's version is the clearest: 'given its form, just as / transparency is by light, by a darkness'. Other English versions are less satisfactory. Wilhelm has 'He takes his state and there he is created, / Diaphanous by light, out of that dark / That comes from Mars'. Pound shows a similar lack of understanding in both versions: 'it takes its state / Formed like a diafan from light on shade / Which shadow cometh from Mars' (1934); 'Formed there in manner as a mist of light / Upon a dusk that is come from Mars and stays' (1928).

Line 18: la qual da Marte vène: Mars, the god of war, reminiscent of the type of Love described in the poems of part 3.

e fa dimora: 'and resides', a clause which is connected to the opening of the stanza: 'In that part where memory is found, Love takes form, just as …., and there resides'.

Lines 19-20: elli è creato: 'Love is created'. This seems to repeat the previous description. As an *accidente*, Love is given form and therefore comes into being in the individual.

ha sensato nome: 'a sensate name' (Nelson). The name is sensate because it is defined in relation to the soul and heart of the individual.

d'alma costume e di cor volontate: 'it is a property of the soul, and an intention of the heart'. As a passion, Love pertains to the sensitive appetite of the soul, found in the heart. Love is created, and takes a sensate name, thanks to a property which pre-exists in the soul, and a will or desire which pre-exists in the heart of the individual.

Again the translations reveal a variety of interpretations and the difficulty of bringing such material over in a concise manner in English. Nelson has 'It is created and has a sensate name, / Is a habit of the soul and an intention of the heart'; Wilhelm, 'And once he's made, he has a name sensate, / Taking desire from heart, from mind his mark'; Goldin, 'It is created out of something seen, / the soul's disposition, and the heart's desire'; Pound, 'Love is created, hath a sensate name, / His modus takes from soul, from heart his will' (1928); and, 'Created, having a name sensate, / Custom of the soul, will from the heart' (1934).

Lines 21-28: Guido tackles the second question, **chi lo fa creare**.

Line 21: Vèn da veduta forma che s'intende: although not a substance in itself, Love is perceived where it exists in an object. This **veduta forma** (seen object) is almost always in Cavalcanti and the poetry of the day, a beautiful lady whom the narrator lays eyes on. **Che s'intende**: an object which the senses of the individual perceive. This allows Love to enter the individual through the eyes, that is 'a seen form that becomes intelligible' (Nelson).

Lines 22-23: these lines explain the meaning of **che s'intende**. The image, itself an *accidente*, 'takes up place and dwelling' (Nelson) in the possible intellect, just as an *accidente* might take the form of any subject.

Line 22: possible intelletto: this is an Aristotelian term to describe the highest seat of the intellect, the ideal intellect, or rationality. See Savona for a further discussion.

Line 24: In quella parte non ha mai possanza: Love, as a passion of the sensitive soul, has no power and no sway in the ideal intellect. Inversely this means that the cognitive processes are incapable of grasping Love. Even though the form Love takes can be evoked by memory as an image (the **veduta forma**), it remains an abstract idea.

Lines 25-28: these lines explain why Love has no power in the possible intellect. The subject changes from Love to the possible intellect, a shift which is difficult to grasp initially due to the similar negative construction in the second hemistiches of lines 24 and 25. Nelson offers a useful description of the possible intellect as presented by Cavalcanti: 'for the very reason that it does not derive from *qualitas* or accidentality, it shines itself as an everlasting effect... Since the possible intellect receives only *intelligibilia* and not *sensibilia*, it does not feel pleasure but rather it contemplates. What it contemplates are the "abstracted" images transmitted by the active intellect which are called *species intelligibiles*' (Nelson). Because it contemplates (**ha ... consideranza**), it cannot construct a term of paragon, and it is therefore impossible to come up with an analogy for Love (De Robertis).

Stanza 3

Lines 29-34: Guido addresses question three: **qual sia sua vertute.**

Line 29: **Non è vertute**: 'it is not a virtue'. In scholasticism **virtute** is a human faculty, as are '*intellectus, voluntas, fantasia, extimativa, memoria et virtus sensitiva comunis et particularis et appetitus sensitivus*' (Dino del Garbo). Nelson, in fact, translates **vertute** with the term 'faculty'.

ma da quella vène: 'but it derives from a virtue'.

Lines 30-31: these lines specify the nature of that virtue. The emphasis is on its sensitive nature (**che sente**), in opposition to rationality (**razionale**). Love is a physical passion.

Line 32: **for di salute giudicar mantene**: 'outside the bounds of sanity and physical health Love pushes good judgement'. It is a rather contorted construction, as often in this poem, as a result of the requirements of the metre. We might paraphrase as follows, 'Love, while it lasts, impedes our use of reason'.

Line 33: ché la 'ntenzione per ragione vale: 'since desire (**intenzione**) takes the place of / imposes itself upon (**vale**) reason'.

Line 34: discerne male in cui è vizio amico: '[indeed] he who (**in cui**) is dominated by vice/excess of passion (**vizio è amico**) is incapable of good judgement (**discerne male**), [since passion and reason are always at odds].

All the English versions differ from my own interpretation here, which is based on De Robertis and Savona. Rather than the indefinite 'one', other translators into English maintain Love as the subject of line 34, leading to awkward results. Nelson has 'It discriminates poorly for one to whom vice is a friend'; Wilhelm, 'Choosing poorly friends to vice's way'; Pound, 'Poor in discernment, being thus weakness' friend' (1928 and 1934).

Lines 35-42: addresses the fourth question: **qual sia... sua potenza.**

Line 35: Di sua potenza segue spesso morte: 'The power of Love is such that it often results in death for the lover'.

Line 36: se forte: a Latinism for 'each time that, or whenever' and not the adverb *fortemente* (Contini).

Lines 36-37: la vertù fosse impedita / la quale aita la contraria via: 'that virtue [vital virtue] which takes the contrary path [to death] is obstructed'. Pound has 'Be it withstayed / and so swinging counterweight' (1934) and 'Be he withstayed / or from true course / bewrayed' (1928).

Line 38: non perché oppost' a naturale sia: 'Not because [Love] is opposed to [human] nature'. Pound has 'Not that it were natural opposite' (1934), which makes of **naturale** an adjective rather than a noun, and renders the phrase incomprehensible.

Line 39: ma quanto che da buon perfetto tort'è: 'but in so far as (**ma quanto che**) [whoever] is deviated (**tort'è**) from the perfect good (**da buon perfetto**)'. The **buon perfetto** is the Aristotelian *bonum perfectum*, to which all human beings should aspire for happiness.

This and the following lines have the impersonal 'whoever' or 'one' as subject, a construction common in Cavalcanti. Pound's second version, which is more accurate in general than his 1928 translation, is nevertheless astray because it maintains Love as the subject.

Line 40: **per sorte, non pò dire om ch'aggia vita**: 'cannot claim to be one who is alive'. The presence of **per sorte** at the beginning of the line offers some difficulties for interpretation. I tend to agree with De Robertis, for whom **per sorte** corresponds (and responds) to **se forte**, and should be linked to the phrase introduced by **quanto che'**.

Line 41: **ché stabilita non ha segnoria**: 'since he has not got a stable (**stabilita**) control (**segnoria**) over himself and his actions'.

Line 42: **A simil pò valer quand'om l'oblia**: 'similarly the same result occurs when one forgets it [the perfect good]'. I agree with De Robertis who suggests the 'it' of this line refers not to Love, as many commentators would have it, but the **buon perfetto** of line 39.

Stanza 4

Lines 43-49: these lines address the fifth question: **qual sia... L'essenza [d'Amore]**. The neat division which has seen each of the eight questions correspond to the formal structure of the canzone breaks down slightly here. Seven lines, rather than the six lines of the *fronte*, are used to form the syntactical unit. Moreover the discussion of the essence of Love could be said to be covered in the first *piede*, while the second, opening with the verb **Move**, already anticipates the material of the *sirima* directed at the sixth question.

Lines 43-44: the narrator tells us quite directly that the essence of Love can be recognised in the unsettling and excessive nature of this insatiable desire.

L'essere: is synonymous with *essenza* (used in line 12), 'essence'.

lo voler è tanto / ch'oltra misura di natura torna: 'desire is such [is so intense] that it exceeds (**torna**) the just limits of nature'.

Line 45: **poi non s'adorna di riposo mai**: 'after which [that is, having exceeded nature's limits] it is never accompanied by (**non s'adorna**

di) rest'. In other words, once desire has exceeded the just limits set by nature, the individual can never again find harmony in love. Nelson has 'In that it never takes refreshment in rest'. Pound has 'He comes to be and is when will's so great / It twists itself from out all natural measure; / Leisure's adornment puts he then never on' (1928), with little variation in the later version.

Lines 46-49: these lines contain a list of some of Love's characteristics.

Line 46: **Move**: 'Transforms'.

cangiando color, riso in pianto: 'causing change of colour, and of laughter into tears'.

Line 47: **e la figura con paura storna**: according to Contini fear causes the figure to turn away from (**storna**) the loved object; similarly Nelson, 'And through fear it puts the image to flight'. But, of course, **figura** could also be the countenance of the lover, which is transformed by fear. This was the interpretation given by Shaw (and more recently Savona and De Robertis): 'now there is a conflict of emotions shown in the changing colour of the lover and the alteration of *riso in pianto*. The lover's face is disfigured with fear' (Shaw 66). Similarly Wilhelm has 'Twisting the face with fear'; and Pound, 'Contorting the face with fear' (1934).

Line 48: **soggiorna**: Love is always changing state, as line 50 reaffirms.

ancor: 'even though'. Lines 48-49 might therefore read: 'Although it doesn't remain in one place for long, one finds Love more often in people of valour'.

Lines 50-56: these lines treat the sixth question concerning the changes in Love, **ciascun suo movimento**.

Line 50: **La nova qualità**: refers to the ever-changing, inconstant nature of Love, which lines 46-49 describe. As a result, it causes sighs (**move sospiri**).

Line 51: **e vol ch'om miri 'n non formato loco**: 'And it desires that one gaze upon an unformed object' (Nelson). The meaning is difficult to determine. Perhaps, as Nelson says, 'in the absence of the lady the lover is forced to feed his love by recourse to his memory and its imperfect image'.

Line 53: imaginar nol pote om che nol prova: 'one who has not experienced it directly cannot imagine the feeling'. The echo in Dante's sonnet 'Tanto gentile' line 11 is noteworthy: 'che 'ntender no la può chi non la prova'.

Line 54: né mova già però ch'a lui si tiri: syntactically complex, **né mova** is connected to line 51: 'Love requires that one gaze upon an unformed object … and that one not move or find distraction from, or take ones allegiance away from, the above mentioned object'.

Line 55: e non si giri per trovarvi gioco: 'and that one not look elsewhere to find relief or pleasure (**gioco**)'.

Line 56: né certamente gran saver né poco: 'or, certainly, to find wisdom of great or small proportion'. Pound (1928, and 1934 is similar) interprets differently, 'Love doth not move, but draweth all to him;/ Nor doth he turn / for a whim / to find delight / Nor to seek out, surely / great knowledge or slight'.

Stanza 5

Lines 57-62: deal with the seventh question, **e 'l piacimento che 'l fa dire amare.**

Line 57: De simil tragge complessione sguardo: 'Love provokes (**tragge**) a glance from a person whose temperament is similar to that of the lover'.

Line 58: che fa parere lo piacere certo: 'which ensures the certainty of pleasure'.

Line 59: non pò coverto star, quand'è sì giunto: 'Love cannot remain hidden (**coverto**) when it reaches this point'.

Line 60: Non già selvagge le bieltà son dardo: the difficulty of this line lies in the meaning of **selvagge**. Savona suggests the term should be read in opposition to **gente di valor**, and therefore as meaning, 'ignoble beauty is no arrow to Love'. Nelson has 'Beauties, but not uncouth ones, are an arrow'. Pound has 'Beautys be darts tho' not savage' (1934).

Line 61: ché tal volere per temere è sperto: 'For such longing is dispelled by fearing' (Nelson).

Line 62: consiegue merto spirito ch'è punto: 'whoever (**spirito**) is struck by such a dart receives what he deserves'.

Lines 63-70: answer the eighth and final question, **s'omo per veder lo pò mostrare**.

Line 63: E non si pò conoscer per lo viso: 'Love is not itself visible' (even though at line 59 we were told that the manifestation of its presence in the complexion of the lover cannot be hidden).

Line 64: compriso: 'once comprehended by the sensitive soul'.

bianco in tale obietto cade: for a discussion of this line and the issue of colour, transparency and light in the poem, see Ardizzone 47-70.

Line 65: e, chi ben aude, forma non si vede: 'and, as one (**chi**) of understanding knows well, form is not visible'. Not, as Pound has it, 'Who heareth, seeth not form / But is led by its emanation' (1934).

aude: a Latinism meaning 'hear'.

Line 66: dunqu' elli meno, che da lei procede: 'much less, therefore, Love which comes (**procede**) from seen form'. Nelson's annotation is useful at this point, 'Since Love cannot be known by sight and since form (in the abstract philosophical sense) is invisible, Love which derives from form is even "more" invisible'. The reasons for this invisibility are described in lines 67-68.

Line 67: For di colore, d'essere diviso: 'devoid of colour, without its own being'. Love is without being in so far as it is an *accidente* and not a *sustanzia* (line 2).

Line 68: assiso 'n mezzo scuro, luce rade: 'situated in (**assiso 'n**) darkness, Love eliminates (**rade**) light'.

Lines 69-70: these two lines offer a summary before the envoi. The verb in the first person singular introduces the change in tone, and reinforces the note of irony implicit in these lines.

Line 69: For d'ogne fraude dico, degno in fede: 'without any trickery I declare, as one worthy of trust'.

Line 70: che solo di costui nasce mercede: 'that only from Love is mercy born'. Both De Robertis and Savona detect a significant amount of irony in this last phrase, and it is difficult to read it otherwise, given the damning presentation of Love which the canzone has just offered: a conception based on negatives, one that destroys reason and pushes the lover into the extremes of passion. Neither of Pound's translations transmit a sense of irony. In the 1934 versions he has 'Being divided, divided from all falsity / Worthy of trust / From him alone mercy proceedeth'.

Congedo

Lines 71-75: It comes as something of a relief to arrive at the clarity of the *congedo* - a final farewell to the canzone, in which the narrator addresses the poem itself and gives advice on the type of audience to seek out and those readers who should be avoided. There is very little that needs annotation. It is worth noting the adjective used to describe the canzone, **adornata**: the poem is adorned with technical accomplishment. Also of note is the distinction made between those poeple who **hanno intendimento** and those who don't. This is similar to the *conoscente* of line 5, which referred to those people of noble spirit and apt in reasoning who will understand the canzone. Pound's 1928 translation closes with that most important rhyme of English love poetry, 'fire' and 'desire': 'So he have sense or glow with reason's fire, / To stand with other hast thou no desire'.

PART SIX: OTHER LOVES?

19 – *Una giovane donna di Tolosa*
20 – *Era in penser d'amor quand'i' trovai*
21 – *In un boschetto trova pasturella*

The poems in part 6 all describe the narrator's encounters with women other than the *donna mia* of the majority of his poetry.

The first composition, 'Una giovane donna di Tolosa', tells how the narrator has been struck with love by a lady from Toulouse, who closely resembles his own lady ('la donna mia'). The metaphysical dimension of love, common to Cavalcanti's other love poetry, is equally at the fore here. The lover's own lady has no monopoly in her ability to destroy him. The Toulousian woman offers a pretext for Cavalcanti to develop yet another variation on the irrational nature of love.

The second and third poems are unusual because they follow, to varying degrees, the genre known as the *pastourelle* (in Italian *pastorella*), wherein an aristocratic male courts favours in love from a country girl. The third poem 'In un boschetto trovai pasturella' fits firmly into this genre.

In Favati's ordering, 'In un boschetto trovai pasturella' is hidden away amongst the correspondence sonnets. But it is important to consider it alongside the second poem here, 'Era in pensar d'amor quand'i' trovai'. The narrator's interlocutors are now two *foresette*, or country girls. This immediately suggests the *pastorella* genre. However, while the poem does include some of the characteristics one finds in 'In un boschetto trovai pasturella', Cavalcanti confuses the expectations of the reader in the conversation between the narrator and the *foresette*.

The title 'Other Loves?' may refer to poems which treat a different woman from the *donna mia* of so many of Guido's poems, but the title is also a question. What do we know of this lady, or ladies? Almost nothing. There is no indication that the lady in the majority of Cavalcanti's poems is one and the same, or even that an attempt, *post factum*, was made to give that appearance, as in Dante and Petrarch. It is not surprising that we know so little of the women who inspired Cavalcanti's poetry, because on the whole his poetry is so self-absorbed. It is the effects that Love and the love object have on the individual and their ability to disrupt the normal workings of rationality that take centre stage.

19 *UNA GIOVANE DONNA DI TOLOSA*

This sonnet is traditionally considered to refer to an incident en route to Santiago de Compostella, to which we know Cavalcanti travelled. The journey is one of the few biographical indications we have for Guido. In his *Cronica* (I xx) Dino Compagni describes how Corso Donati attempted to assassinate Guido en route. Whether Cavalcanti arrived as far as Santiago is unknown and insignificant. He did, it seems, reach Toulouse where he was love-struck by a *giovane donna*. Her name, if we are to believe the narrator himself, was Mandetta, for she is referred to directly in the next ballad, 'Era in penser d'amor quand'i' trovai', which speaks of the same event.

The experience of divided allegances to Love was a common topos. Take, for example, the *Vita Nuova*, particularly the five chapters dedicated to an analogous experience, XXXV-XXXIX, in which, some time after the death of Beatrice, Dante notices 'una gentile donna giovane e bella molto'. Cavalcanti presents the confusion over love-objects with a hint of irony. But no attempt is made to resolve the situation. Here the difference from the analogous episode in *Vita Nuova* is revealing.

There are translations by Rossetti (VII. Sonnet: Of the Eyes of a Certain Mandetta, of Thoulouse, which resemble those of his Lady Joan, of Florence) and Pound (1912).

STRUCTURAL NOTE
The rhyme scheme of this sonnet is ABAB ABAB CDE DCE. The first quatrain describes the new lady, only to return to the lady of the lover's

heart in the fourth line. This is paralleled in the first tercet. The second quatrain and tercet are both dedicated to describing the movements of the narrator's *anima*. De Robertis notes the new lady occupies lines 1 and 14 – the external parts – while the narrator's original love occupies the important internal lines, especially at the close of both quatrains and the first tercet.

All six lines in the sestet are *a minore* in structure with secondary ictus on the 8th metrically relevant syllable. In the octet, too, the *a minore* line clearly predominates.

ANNOTATIONS

Line 2: gentil: 'noble in spirit, of high moral worth'.

onesta: 'honourable'.

leggiadria: 'grace and comeliness'. Nelson has 'elegance'. Pound has 'quaint sincerities', and his version of the quatrain as a whole gives little sense of how the woman made an impression on the narrator: 'The grace of youth in Toulouse ventureth; / She's noble and fair, with quaint sincerities, / Direct she is and is about her eyes / Most like to our Lady of sweet memories'. Rossetti has 'cheerful modesty' at this point.

Line 3: e dritta e simigliante: hendiadys for 'perfectly'.

Line 4: dolci occhi: echoed in line 9 with 'dolce sguardo'.

della donna mia: In the translation I have used lady as a perfect rhyme in lines 1 and 3, though the word refers to the two different women.

Line 5-6: the same process of the soul leaving the heart is described in detail in poem 7. The comparison with Dante's 'Gentil pensero che parla di vui', from the *Vita Nuova*, is also interesting. There the soul, which is explicitly identified with reason or intellect by Dante, is the last bastion resisting the assault by the image of the lady, and tries to convince the heart (identified in turn with the appetites) to resist. In Dantean terms Cavalcanti is already lost, because the image of the lady has touched both body and soul, and no part of the narrator is able to resist.

Lines 5-8: for the translator into English this quatrain is difficult because of the confusion over pronouns. 'Soul' in Italian is feminine, while 'heart' is masculine. But, since the lady is also an actor in this quatrain, it is hard to distinguish between the soul and the lady if both are referred to as 'she'. I have therefore taken the liberty of referring to the soul in this poem, and this poem alone, with the masculine pronoun. The other alternative might have been to use 'it', as Rossetti and Nelson do, but the dramatic effect of the personification is lessened in that case. Pound, too, uses the masculine pronoun.

Line 5: disiderosa: 'desirous', adopted by Pound and Nelson. Rossetti has 'sweet desire'.

Line 6: in guisa che: 'in such a manner that…'

da lui si svia: 'the soul leaves the heart'.

Line 7: e vanne a lei: the soul goes (metaphorically, of course) to be with the new lady. Pound, playing on the fact that Guido was supposedly on a pilgrimage, has 'She [the Lady] has clad the soul in fashions peregrine'.

Line 9: Quella: the difficulty discussed above, relating to multiple grammatical subjects of the one gender, becomes an interpretative problem in the Italian, since the demonstrative pronoun could refer either to the lady or the soul. De Robertis considers that it refers to the soul, as do Nelson and Pound. Cassata and Rossetti read the lady as subject.

la mira: 'fixes in her gaze'. See also the opening line of poem 2.

Line 11: v'è dentro: in the eyes of the new lady the soul sees an identical image of Love to that in his own lady.

donna dritta: the adjective echoes line 3.

Line 13: tagliente dardo: literally 'a cutting dart', sharp enough to wound him mortally.

20 ERA IN PENSER D'AMOR QUAND'I' TROVAI

In this ballad reference is made to the narrator's meeting with the lady of Toulouse in the previous sonnet. Hence, the incident offers editors a rare occasion to order a poem on the basis of internal links. According to the fiction of the ballad, the narrator now recounts that meeting to 'due foresette nove', two country girls, whom he meets by chance. Importantly these girls are not *donne*. As members of a lower social class they would not traditionally be considered to inspire noble love. Such meetings between writer and country girl were described within the genre of the *pastourelle*. The next poem, 'In un boschetto' is an excellent example. The meeting here, however, is different from a traditional *pastourelle*. Cavalcanti speaks with the two girls at length, describing his love for the Toulousian lady, while they in turn pity his situation and offer advice. There is no suggestion of a sexual encounter. Guido also wrote a second ballad describing his love and *sbigottimento* for one of the two *foresette*, 'Gli occhi di quella gentil foresetta'. In both the *foresette* ballads there is something of a transgression of literary norms. Here they are described as 'cortese e umìle', and as carrying 'la chiave di ciascuna vertù alta e gentile', attributes normally reserved for the *donna mia*. This led De Robertis to suggest that the meeting offers a starting point for Dante's important encounter with 'donne che hanno intelletto d'amore' in chapter XVIII of the *Vita Nuova*.

But while this new encounter does seem to open the way for another variation on the narrator's suffering and *sbigottimento*, there are some important differences. However much Guido subverts the *pastorella* genre by giving the girls noble qualities and limiting the conversation to his love for the *donna di Tolosa*, there is a certain casualness about the encounter, a lightness of tone and a relaxed style of narration that is new to the corpus. We notice this change in the opening sentence with its stock phrase from the *pastorella* genre. But it is also evident in the fact that this ballad and the next are the only two poems in the corpus in which the narrator interacts directly with a woman in the course of the narration. For the first time, he engages in dialogue and makes an attempt to bring the woman to life as a character. Normally the lady is absent, and somewhat abstract, so that she takes on the significance of a metaphysical Absence, allowing the narrator to focus on his own psyco-physical responses. Even in the poem describing his love for one of the *foresette*, 'Gli occhi di quella gentil foresetta', Cavalcanti reverts to this practice (one could replace *foresetta* with *donna* in the first line without any disruption). If this ballad is to be considered a *pastourelle*, then it seems audacious of Cavalcanti to end the poem with a *congedo* in which he describes the fictionalized intention that it should find its way to the lady of Toulouse.

Versions exist by Pound (1912, published 1920), and Rossetti (VIII. Ballata: He reveals, in a Dialogue, his increasing Love for Mandetta). Both Rossetti and Pound followed Italian editions in which stanza 5 was placed between stanzas 2 and 3.

STRUCTURAL NOTE

This *ballata mezzana* of 52 lines is by far the longest surviving ballad Cavalcanti wrote. There are six eight line stanzas and a four line refrain. Two *mutazioni* in hendecasyllables rhyme AB. These are followed by a *volta* that rhymes Bccx, made up of one hendecasyllable and three *settenari*. Each stanza has the following rhyme pattern, ABAB Bccx. The refrain follows the pattern of the *volta*. Generally a refrain of four lines would lead to the appellation *ballata grande*, but because only one of these lines is a hendecasyllable it is called a *ballata mezzana*. There is a large amount of direct speech, which closes every stanza, and which, in stanzas 1, 3, 4 and 5, begins in line 3.

ANNOTATIONS

Line 1: **Era in penser d'amor**: this is a standard opening phrase in the *pastourelle* genre. See De Robertis for other examples.

Line 2: **foresette**: this is the diminutive form of *forese*, meaning 'peasant', or 'rural labourer'. Nelson has 'little country girls'; Rossetti, 'youthful damozels'; and Pound, 'damsels strange' (though in line 9 Pound has 'little maids' and in line 38 'Maid o' the wood'). It is interesting that there should be two. De Robertis suggests that this fact distances the encounter from the traditional expectations of the *pastourelle* genre.

nove: 'young'.

Line 3: **E' piove**: 'It is raining'.

Line 4: **gioco**: 'gioia'. **Gioco d'amore** is a periphrasis for 'love'. Rossetti has 'One sung: "Our life inhales / All love continually;"' Pound, 'The rains / of love are falling, falling within us'.

Line 5: vista: 'appearance'.

soave: this is the first of a series of adjectives that describe the two *foresette* in terms traditionally adopted for people of nobility. Rossetti has 'Their aspect was so utterly serene, / so courteous, of such quiet nobleness'; Pound, 'So quiet in their modest courtesies / Their aspect coming softly on my vision'; and Nelson, 'The sight of them was so pleasant / and so calm, courteous, and benevolent'.

Line 9: Deh: an interjection. See poem 7.

no m'abbiate a vile: 'do not hold me in disdain'. **Vile** is in opposition to **gentile** in the previous line. The use by Guido of **vile** to describe himself, and **gentile** to describe the *foresette*, is another reversal of expectations, possibily to emphasise his *sbigottimento* for the *donna di Tolosa*.

Line 10: colpo: 'wound'. The word is repeated at lines 16 and 23.

Line 14: che vider come 'l cor era ferito: the two women turn towards the narrator and observe his heart. This had been anticipated in line 11, **questo core**, 'this heart here before you'. This image recurs in line 23, **'L tuo colpo, che nel cor si vede**. The same theme appears in poem 12, line 13, where the ostentation is linked to a suggestion of martyrdom.

Line 15: un spiritel nato di pianto: a circumlocution for 'tears'.

Line 17: sbigottito: see the discussion in the introduction to part 3.

Line 18: che rise: the laughter is not a sign of disdain or irony, but rather an expression of happiness that Love has triumphed over the lover (De Robertis). I have followed Pound in translating 'smile' rather than 'laugh'. Similarly in line 22, the other woman is transformed by joy into a figure of Love, **fatta di gioco in figura d'Amore**. Despite Cavalcanti's downtrodden state, both women interpret his love in positive terms, as lines 23-28 and lines 39-44 reveal.

Lines 19-20: 'Look how he is won by the strength of love.'

Line 22: fatta di gioco in figura d'amore: the girl is an image or personification of love. Pound has 'Fashioned for pleasure in love's fashioning'; Rossetti, 'Fashioned for sport in Love's own image'.

Line 24: tratto: 'inflicted'.

d'occhi di troppo valore: the eyes of the lady have overwhelmed the lover. The importance of the eyes in the process of love is repeated in the narrator's description of the *donna di Tolosa* at lines 34-36, and again by the other *foresetta* at lines 40-42.

Line 32: accordellata istretta: this describes the dress of the *donna di Tolosa* as being narrow at the waist, or possibly tied at the waist. Nelson has 'tightly laced'; Pound, 'in a corded bodice'; Rossetti, 'sweetly kirtled and enlaced'.

Line 33: Amor la qual chiamava la Mandetta: 'which lady was called Mandetta by Love'. **Mandetta** was probably a diminutive form of the common first name, Amande.

Line 35: che fin dentro, a la morte: 'profoundly, even to the point of causing death'. Death is used repeatedly in the poems of part 3 as the extreme point of suffering. Nelson has 'She arrived so briskly and forcefully / That her eyes struck me, / Deep within, to death'; Pound, 'A lightning swift to fall, / And naught within recall / Save, Death! My wounds! Her eyes!'; and Rossetti, 'Yea, by her eyes indeed / My life has been decreased / To death inevitably'.

Line 44: raccomàndati a lui: 'beseech him [Love]'.

Line 45: Vanne: 'Go'.

ballatetta: see poem 22, line 2, where the same diminutive form is used.

Line 46: quetamente: 'humbly' or 'reverently'.

la Dorata: this is the name of a church in Toulouse where the ballad might be expected to encounter Mandetta. The church, known as the Daurade because of its gilded frescos, was completely rebuilt in later centuries; there is still a church on the same site on the Garonne River today.

Line 47-48: 'And here ask of some courteous lady if you may be brought before..'.

Line 51: leve: 'light' or 'soft'.

Line 52: Per: 'In the hope of receiving'.

21 *IN UN BOSCHETTO TROVA' PASTURELLA*

This ballad is a *pastourelle*, a composition common in early French, *langue d'oïl*, though also used by Provençal poets. A *pastourelle* was narrated by a traveller, often a knight, and always male, who describes an encounter with a country girl which was normally sexual. The narrator might sometimes be humiliated, or the shepherdess make her escape, but more often than not the tale would end to the advantage of the traveller, who may or may not have gained the girl's consent before his objective was reached. The scene was generally rustic. The *pastourelle* described a love that was radically different to the *fino amore* normally occupying thirteenth-century poets. Difference in class seems to have been an important factor in making possible the transgression of social boundaries. Whereas in poem 19 Guido was quick to identify the woman as a *donna*, or lady, here she is identified in the first line as a *pasturella*. Poem 20 is particularly interesting because it confuses these traditional distinctions.

This ballad follows the stylised content of the genre. It is worth noting, however, that the representation of the woman does not simply identify her as a sexual object, but as a figure of beauty worthy of praise similar to that reserved for the *donna* of other poems.

The refrain, 'più che la stella bella, al mi parere', reveals a debt to Guinizzelli, 'Io voglio del ver la mia donna laudare' [I want to praise my lady truly], line 3 of which reads 'più che stella diana splende e pare' [more than the morning star she appears and shines]. In Guinizzelli's sonnet 'Chi vedesse a Lucia un var capuzzo' [Seeing Lucy draw a hood of fur], elements of the *pastorella* can also be found: 'Ah!, prender lei a forza, ultra su' grato, / e bagiarli la bocca e 'l bel visaggio / e li occhi suoi, ch' èn due fiamme de foco' [Oh, to take her by force, against her will / and kiss her mouth and her beautiful face / and her eyes, which are two flames of fire].

A shepherdess named Pastorella appears in Spenser's *The Faerie Queene*

(Book 6, Cantos 9-12). The genre was common throughout Europe, and continued to find expression in later periods, too. Keats's 'La belle dame sans merci' has a radically different sentimental turn, but it adopts many of the linguistic and descriptive keys present in this and earlier *pastourelles*:

> I met a Lady in the Meads,
> Full beautiful, a faery's child,
> Her hair was long, her foot was light
> And her eyes were wild.
>
> I made a Garland for her head,
> And bracelets too, and fragrant Zone;
> She looked at me as she did love
> And made sweet moan.

The ballad is accompanied in the Chigiano L.VIII, 305 codex by a satirical sonnet thought to have been written by Lapo degli Uberti. The sonnet insinuates that Guido's *pasturella* was in fact 'un bel pastore'.

> *Guido, quando dicesti pasturella,*
> *vorre' ch' avessi dett' un bel pastore:*
> *ché si conven, ad om che vogli onore,*
> *contar, se pò, verace sua novella.*
> * Tuttor verghett' avea piacente e bella:*
> *per tanto lo tu' dir non ha fallore,*
> *ch'i' non conosco re né 'mperadore*
> *che non l'avesse agiat' a camerella.*
> * Ma dicem' un, che fu tec' al boschetto*
> *il giorno che sì pasturav' agnelli,*
> *che non s'avide se non d'un valletto*
> * che cavalcava ed era biondetto*
> *ed avea li suo' panni corterelli.*
> *Però rasetta, se vuo', tuo motetto.*

My own translation is as follows.

> Guido, that shepherd girl you wrote about,
> I wish you'd said she was a pretty boy,
> for men of honour shouldn't toy
> with truth when telling how things were.
>   It's true this person's crook was, as you write,
> pleasing to the eye and soundly formed,
> and even a Bishop or two, I've been informed,
> could verify accounts of that sweet sight.
>   But I'm told by one who was with you on that day
> how in that wood and tending sheep was none
> other than a blonde-haired boy who played
>   at riding like a squire – most skillfully done
> considering his pants were down about his knees:
> so do be brave enough to fix your ballad, please.

There are versions by Rossetti (XXI. Ballata: Concerning a Shepherd-maid), and Pound (1912). Three other versions exist by Goldin, Fraser, and Wilhelm. This makes the ballad one of the most frequently translated into English of all Cavalcanti's poems. Rossetti's version stands out for its ability to confront the theme with a control of language that avoids falling into doggerel and clichés. This is perhaps the greatest difficulty for the translator of 'In un boschetto', because the language is so stylised. How does one translate a line like 'più che la stella bella, al mi' parere', or 'Cavelli avea biondetti e ricciutelli', while making it come alive as poetry?

STRUCTURAL NOTE
Because the ballad has a two line refrain it is known as a *ballata minore*. This is followed by four stanzas of six lines, AB AB BX, where X rhymes with the second line of the refrain. In addition to the end rhymes, there is a *rima al mezzo* in the last line of each stanza which adopts the rhyme-sound of B. (The rima al mezzo describes a rhyme that comes at the end of the

first hemistich; in any other position it is simply an internal rhyme.) This playful device is not uncommon in Cavalcanti; 'Donna me prega' is the most famous *Duecento* example.

ANNOTATIONS

Lines 1 and 2: Opening refrain: the opening refrain contains both a *rima al mezzo* and an internal rhyme in the second line. Pound has 'In wood-way found I once a shepherdess, / More fair than stars are was she to my seeming'. Nelson writes 'In a little wood I found a shepherdess / More beautiful than the stars, so I think'. Rossetti has 'Within a copse I met a shepherd-maid / More fair, I said, than any star to see'.

Spenser's famous refrain in 'Prothalamion' is a good example in English of a seeminly simply phrase that works as memorable poetry, 'Sweete *Themmes* runne softly, till I end my Song'.

Line 1: the opening is a standard trope in this stylised genre. It would have alerted the reader to the type of poem to follow.

trova': literally 'I found'.

Line 2: più che la stella bella: the singular is used in place of the plural to facilitate the rhyme.

Line 4: cera: 'face' or 'features'.

Line 5: verghetta: 'shepherd's staff'. I have not included this in my translation as it does not add anything to the description of the shepherdess or her activity, and nothing else in the ballad suggests that it should be read metaphorically, as Lapo degli Uberti would have it.

Line 6: [di]scalza: 'barefooted'.

Line 7: song, especially a song of love, is traditionally that which alerts the knight to the presence of the shepherdess. The phrase is echoed in the opening line of *Purgatorio* XXIX, 'Cantando come donna innamorata'.

Line 8: di tutto piacere: 'joy' or 'beauty'. Rossetti has 'and fashioned for all ecstasy'. Pound has 'And joy was on her for an ornament'.

Line 9: D'amor la saluta imantenente: 'I greeted her amorously without delay'.

Line 12: sola sola: 'all alone'.

gia: 'was wandering'.

Line 13: pia: 'sings or chirps'.

Line 14: drudo: 'partner' or 'lover'.

Line 17: or è stagione: 'now is the moment'.

Line 18: di questa pasturella gio' pigliare: Nelson has 'to have joy of this shepherdess'. Rossetti employs a circumlocution, "Even now then', said my thought, 'the time recurs, / With mine own longing to assuage her mood". Pound has: 'And thought me how 't was but the time's provision / to gather joy of this small shepherd maid'.

Line 19: Merzé le chiesi: 'I asked her permission'.

Line 23: menòmmi sott'una freschetta foglia: i.e. 'into the shade of the trees', or, in Keats's words, 'She took me to her elfin grot'.

Line 25: gioia e dolzore: synonyms for 'joy', or 'pleasure'. The second noun is not *dolore*, but *'dolcezza'*. Pound ends his translation with a rhyming couplet: 'And there I drank in so much summer sweetness / Meseemed Love's god connived at its completeness'. Rossetti has 'And on that day, by Joy's enchanting art, / There Love in very presence seemed to be'.

Line 26: parea: the same verb is found in the opening refrain.

PART SEVEN: EXILE AND EPILOGUE

22 – *Perch'i' no spero di tornar giammai*
23 – *Noi siàn le triste penne isbigotite*

The two poems in this last part are not found together in previous ordering. At first this particular ballad and sonnet may not seem to have much in common, aside from both sharing thematic links with the poems in part 3. What they do share, and what makes them remarkable in Cavalcanti's corpus, is the motif of writing. The process of writing is brought explicitly to our attention and it results in a greater self-reflection and sophistication. 'Noi siàn le triste penne isbigotite' is addressed to the narrator's writing instruments, while in 'Perch'i' no spero' the narrator addresses the ballad itself, and then, in the *congedo*, the very voice of that ballad. For this reason the present two poems are an appropriate conclusion to our selection. Cavalcanti, led by his spirit of playfulness, has created two of his finest compositions.

22 *PERCH'I' NO SPERO DI TORNAR GIAMMAI*

A *ballatetta* is literally a little ballad, though, as often with the diminutive in Italian, it is used more to refer to the speaker's affection for it than the object's actual size or significance. Indeed this is one of Cavalcanti's more sophisticated poems. The idea is itself ingenious: not the final *congedo*, as tradition would have it, but the entire poem is addressed to the ballad itself, while the closing stanza is addressed to the narrator's own voice.

The popularity of this ballad rests as much on the theme of exile as on its playful spirit. Previously readers had seized upon it as one of the few biographical clues in Guido's poetry and concluded it must refer to his exile, from Florence, to the marsh lands of Sarzana in early 1300. Rossetti, for example, entitles his translation 'In Exile in Sarzana', and places it towards the end of his selection. There is no evidence that the poem actually corresponds to this period. Indeed it appears rather unlikely given that exile and distance from the loved lady was a frequent trope in *Duecento* poetry (and beyond: Shakespeare's sonnet L, for example, 'How heavy do I journey on the way'). Any attempt to trace elements in the poem to the biography of Cavalcanti rests on conjecture. It is more useful to point out the links to other poems by the author. The themes of distance and desperation are prominent in the previous two pieces in Favati's ordering, poem 14, 'Io temo che la mia disaventura' and 'La forte e nova mia disaventura'. The keyword 'disaventura' in both first lines is also found in line 11 of our ballad.

The poem has made an impression on many English-language modernist poets, who most probably took their lead from Ezra Pound. Basil Bunting's second book of odes ends with the poem, 'Now we've no hope of going back', whose epigraph recalls Cavalcanti. More famously T.S.Eliot made use of the opening line in the first poem of his *Ash Wednesday* series entitled, 'Because I do not hope to turn again':

> Because I do not hope to turn again
> Because I do not hope
> Because I do not hope to turn
> Desiring this man's gift and that man's scope
> I no longer strive to strive towards such things
> (Why should the agèd eagle stretch its wings?)
> Why should I mourn
> The vanished power of the usual reign?

The whole poem is inspired by the rhythmic force Eliot perceived in the original, and an attempt to play with its possible translations in English. Interestingly this line has become a fine example of the open-ended nature of translation. Eliot's poem was then translated by Montale. Rather than revert to Cavalcanti's line, Montale produced a further Italian variation,

'Perch'io non spero di tornare ancora'.

There are versions by Rossetti (XXV. Ballata. In Exile at Sarzana) and Pound (1912, with some variations in 1920). There are also poetic translations by Fraser and Wilhelm, and a prose version by Kay.

STRUCTURAL NOTE

This ballad is *stravagante* in form because it has six lines in the opening refrain, Bccddx. The refrain is followed by four stanzas of ten lines each divided into two *mutazioni*, AB, and a *volta* which follows the length and pattern of the refrain.

The last line of the refrain and of each stanza is not linked by rhyme to any other within the stanza, but to the last line of the preceding stanza. Cavalcanti uses this rhyme to reinforce key words for the poem: 'onore', 'dolore', 'core', 'Amore' and 'valore'.

The poem has a playful spirit and lightness, despite the ever present theme of the narrator's suffering. This is in part due to the neat division between hendecasyllables and quicker *settenari* – each ten line stanza has five of the first followed by an equal number of the second. The rhyming couplets in the *settenari* give a particularly sprightly rhythm.

ANNOTATIONS

Line 1: the phrase 'perch'io no spero' is also found in line 6 of poem 18. In both instances it is used in the context of a justification for speaking.

giammai: 'never again'.

Line 2: ballatetta: the diminutive expresses affection, and is also found in poem 20, line 45. The Italian word allows the translation to maintain the alliterative 't' sounds which dominate the whole opening refrain. Nelson and Fraser both have 'little ballad'; Rossetti, simply 'ballad'; while Pound and Wilhelm have also adopted 'Ballatteta'. Kay translates 'little song'.

Line 3: leggera e piana: these two adjectives are difficult to translate because they remain so open in this particular context. A literal translation is obliged to use adjectives such as 'light' and 'soft', which do not resonate in English today. Both adjectives, interestingly, refer to the composition itself – the style of which is, as I have noted with reference to the rhythmic structure, both sprightly and playful. Nelson and Kay are most literal with 'lightly and softly' and 'lightly and quiet', respectively; Rossetti avoids the two adjectives and uses the adverb 'straight' linked to the verb 'go' in the third line; while Pound has 'Light-foot go thou some fleet way / Unto my Lady straightway'. Fraser has 'swift and sleight'.

Line 6: onore: 'welcome'. Rossetti has 'Shall show thee courtesy'; Pound, 'Great honour will she do thee'.

Line 7: novelle: 'news'.

di sospiri: the news is written in sighs.

Line 9: persona non: 'no one'.

ti miri: 'sees or notices you'.

gentil natura: 'nobility of spirit'. See the discussion in relation to poem 1.

Line 11: disaventura: 'misfortune'.

Line 12: contesa: 'misunderstood', or 'misinterpreted', rather than 'challenged' or 'stopped on the way' (De Robertis). Pound, however, has 'Thou wert made prisoner / And held afar from her' at lines 12 and 13.

Line 13: da lei ripresa: refers to the 'persona' of line 9.

Line 14: angoscia: 'cause for anguish'.

Lines 15 and 16: dopo la morte poscia / pianto e novel dolore.: this doesn't refer to a punishment after death, but rather an intensified sense of anguish at the thought that death will not provide the alleviation of suffering which he had hoped.

Line 17: tu: note the repetition of the second person singular pronoun in the opening line of each stanza. The care with which the narrator imparts instructions to the *ballatetta* and the voice are suggested by the emphatic use of the pronoun.

Line 19: 'l cor si sbatte forte: 'is very perturbed'.

Line 20: per quel che: 'as a result of that which the spirits say ('ragiona')'.

Line 21: la mia persona: this is obviously the narrator himself.

Importantly the syntactic construction allows him to objectify himself somewhat.

Line 22: soffrire: 'I can no longer bear this suffering'.

Lines 25 and 26: a literal version might run, '(I beg this of you most adamantly) / when it leaves the heart'. The soul will leave its seat in the heart in order to escape the unbearable suffering. Lines 24-26 are varied only slightly in the opening of the next stanza.

Lines 33-36: the words the *ballatetta* must speak to the lady are similar to those spoken by the writing instruments in lines 12-14 of poem 23.

Line 37: the last stanza functions as a *congedo*. Normally this was marked by the narrator addressing himself directly to the poem. Cavalcanti ingeniously overcomes this hurdle by addressing himself to *la voce*, the 'voice'. It is the narrator's own voice, which 'comes crying from out of the heart', but it is also the voice of the poem, and the distinction between the two is never clearly made.

deboletta: not by chance, this adjective rhymes with 'ballatetta', which is found in the opening line of the previous two stanzas. It is the diminutive of *debole*, 'weak'. Calenda notes how the first four lines of this last stanza not only present the shaken voice, but four other members of the divided person of the narrator which had already appeared in the ballad: 'il cor dolente', the 'anima', the 'ballatetta', and the 'strutta mente' (Calenda 51). Nelson has 'You, dismayed and frail voice'; Pound, 'O smothered voice and weak that tak'st the road'.

Line 38: echoes line 3 of poem 9, 'e li sospir' che manda 'l cor dolente'.

Line 40: della strutta mente: also found in poem 8, line 11: 'sì che del colpo fu strutta la mente'.

23 *NOI SIÀN LE TRISTE PENNE ISBIGOTITE*

The narrator's own writing instruments are adopted for the device of prosopopoeia in this sonnet. It is a sophisticated reflection on the process of writing, and a further step in the narrator's attempt to render himself objectively by giving the objects around him, as earlier his own organs and feelings, a voice of their own. In spirit it is so representative of Cavalcanti that, as De Robertis suggested, it could easily act as epigraph or epilogue to the entire collection of his poetry. I have had no hesitation in taking up this suggestion.

Once again Cavalcanti astonishes with his ability to find new, playful means to express the same themes, to shift the representation of his suffering to the act of writing, and emphasise the fragmentation of the individual not only through his spirits, heart and soul, but the material possessions around him.

There is no version by Rossetti. Pound never published a translation of this sonnet. However, in *Guido Cavalcanti Rime* (1932), he did print the original alone in a section entitled 'Cavalcanti *attribuite*'. Anderson has found a previously unpublished manuscript version dated 1927-31 (Anderson 186-7), and it is to this which I refer. There is also a version by Wilhelm, whose verse translation maintains the rhyme scheme of the original at the expense of much else: lines 5 and 6, for example, read 'We'll tell you why we've camped apart / And come to you, reader, now and here'.

STRUCTURAL NOTE
The rhyme scheme of this sonnet is ABBA ABBA CDE DCE.

ANNOTATIONS
Line 1: **siàn**: here, as elsewhere in the sonnet –*àn* is the apocopated form of –*ano*, which is, in turn, the Florentine desinence for the first person plural –*amo* (De Robertis). The positioning of the verb in the line is paralleled in lines 5 and 12.

isbigotite: 'sbigotite'. See the introduction to part 3 for a discussion of this word.

Lines 1-2: **penne**: 'quills'; **cesoiuzze** and **coltellin**: instruments used to cut and sharpen the quill. These second two are both in the diminutive form, which, as we saw in 'Perch'i no spero', is used to connotate familiarity. Pound has 'The creaking scissors'.

Line 3: dolorosamente: the Italian adverb echoes 'dolente' in line 2. Dolorosamente does not indicate reluctance to perform the writing task, but rather functions within the framework of the metonymy which sees them as an extension of the narrator's pain. Both Wilhelm and Pound choose 'strife' because it rhymes with 'knife'. Pound has 'Who through our grief make strife / Of words'.

Line 4: 'The words which you have heard'. This would seem to refer to another poem. Contini and Tanturli suggest that this sonnet was written to accompany 'I' prego voi che di dolor parlate'. Line 3 of that ballad, 'non disdegniate la mia pena audire', is echoed in the last tercet of this sonnet.

Line 6: di presente: 'in this present moment', or possibly 'into your presence'.

Line 7: la man: the writing hand of the narrator. Here is a further complication, or fragmentation, of the individual – nothing is saved from the process of prosopopoeia. Notice the concentration of verbs in this line. I refer to 'the hand' as 'she', in accordance with gender of *mano* in Italian.

Line 8: cose dubbiose: 'fearful things or sensations'.

apparite: the verb is often used in Cavalcanti in relation either to a manifestation of fear or a materialisation of the narrator's own feelings (De Robertis). In this sense it it similar to the English word 'apparition'.

Line 9: le quali: refers to the apparitions.

sì: emphatic, as it is in line 10.

costui: refers to the heart. The instruments here, as was the case with the voice and the *ballatetta* in the previous ballad, are like ambassadors on a delicate mission – hence the emphasis on travelling, on the pseudo-objective stance the instruments take, and the diplomatic language that suggests rather than explicitly states.

Line 13: tenerci: 'keep us with you'.

Line 14: tanto che: 'in order that', or 'in the hope that'. Nelson and

Pound, however, interpret this phrase as 'for so long as'.

un poco di pietà vi miri: 'a little pity not be displeasing to you'.

NOTES TO THIS SECTION

1. For further discussion see Boyde (1971) pp. 291-6, and Dragonetti pp. 253-4.

2. For further discussion see Beltrami p. 366.

3. For a further discussion see Boyde (1971) pp. 253-4.

4. Quotations and ordering for the poems of Arnaut Daniel come from *Le canzoni di Arnaut Daniel*, a cura di M. Perugi, (Milan, Ricciardi, 1979).

5. There remains Cavalcanti's 'Certe mie rime a te mandar vogliendo', the addressee of which is not known for certain, though many strong indications suggest Dante. See De Robertis.

6. One other sonnet that should be mentioned here is 'Amore e monna Lagia e Guido ed io'. It is now widely considered to be by Dante, and would therefore seem to be concerned with Dante, Cavalcanti, and Lapo Gianni.

7. To speak of a *cobla capfinidas* is not technically correct, since this term, from the Provençal *cobla* equalling stanza, refers to a linguistic repetition or echo between two separate stanzas. The principal is the same, even if we are correctly speaking, in this case, of a link across the two parts of the sonnet.

8. Some scholars, including De Robertis, proposed reading Lippo in place of Lapo on the basis of conflicting manuscripts. This has been refuted more recently. See Cassata for a further discussion.

9. For a general discussion see Cassata, 'La paternale di Guido (Rime XLI)' in *Studi danteschi*, LIII (1981), pp. 167-85, and the relevant entry in the *Enciclopedia dantesca*, III, pp. 536-7.

10. See Contini p. 548, who notes that this argument is supported by the use of *vile* in the *Vita Nuova*, during the chapters concerned with

Beatrice's death.

11. Antonio Pagliaro, 'Il disdegno di Guido', in *Saggi di critica semantica* (Florence, D'Anna, 1961) pp. 372-376.

12. Marti, 'Sulla genesi del realismo dantesco', in *Realismo dantesco e altri studi* (Milan, Ricciardi, 1961) pp. 22-23; Corrado Calenda, *Per altezza d'ingegno* (Napoli, Liguori, 1976) p. 112.

13. See *The Complete Poetical Works of Percy Bysshe Shelley*, ed. by N. Rogers, v.2 1814-1817 (Oxford, Oxford Uuniversity Press, 1975) p. 16; and also T. Webb, *The Violet in the Crucible: Shelley and Translation* (Oxford, Oxford University Press, 1976) pp. 280-283. Although the editor cannot give a precise date for the translation it seems most likely that it was written around 1814. It was not published until 1876, however, meaning that it would not have been known to Rossetti.

14. For a further discussion of such repetition see Chapter 6 of Boyde (1971).

15. For a full discussion of early commentaries of 'Donna me prega', including that by Dino del Garbo and Ficino, see Fenzi.

16. See Zygmunt Baranski, 'Guido Cavalcanti and His First Readers' in *Guido Cavalcanti tra i suoi lettori* for a discussion of early perceptions and portraits of Cavalcanti.

17. See De Robertis for a fuller discussion, and more recently Ardizzone (2002).

18. For a summary of the discussion surrounding the lady, and Corti's suggestion that she represents philosophy, see Savona, pp. 13-16.

SELECT BIBLIOGRAPHY

RECENT ITALIAN EDITIONS OF CAVALCANTI

Branca, Vittore, ed. *Rimatori del Dolce Stil Nuovo*. Ristampa. Milan: Casa Editrice Dante Alighieri, 1965.

Cassata, Letterio, ed. *Rime*. Guido Cavalcanti. Anzio: De Rubeis, 1993.

Ciccuto, Marcello, ed. *Rime*. Guido Cavalcanti. Milan: Rizzoli, 1978.

Contini, Gianfranco, ed. *Poeti del Duecento*. 2 vols. Milan: Ricciardi, 1960.

De Robertis, Domenico, ed. *Rime, con le rime di Iacopo Cavalcanti*. Guido Cavalcanti. Turin: Einaudi, 1986.

Favati, Guido, ed. *Rime*. Guido Cavalcanti. Milan: Ricciardi, 1957.

Marti, Mario, ed. *Poeti del Dolce stil nuovo*. Florence: Le Monnier, 1969.

CAVALCANTI IN ENGLISH

Anderson, David, *Pound's Cavalcanti: An Edition of the Translations, Notes and Essays*. Princeton: Princeton UP, 1983. Contains all Pound's various versions of Cavalcanti.

Cirigliano, Marc, ed. and trans. *Guido Cavalcanti: The Complete Poems*. New York: Italica Press, 1992.

Foster, Kenelm and Boyde, Patrick, eds and trans. *Dante's Lyric Poetry*. 2 volumes. Oxford: OUP, 1967.

Fraser, G.S., *The Traveller Has Regrets*. London: The Harville Press, 1948. Contains versions of poems 21 and 22.

Kay, George R., *The Penguin Book of Italian Verse*. Harmondsworth: Penguin, 1958, revised 1965. Contains prose translations of six poems, including 2 and 22.

Goldin, Frederick, *German and Italian Lyrics of the Middle Ages: An Anthology and a History*. Garden City: Anchor Books, 1973. Prose translations of nine poems including 1, 2, 16, 18, and 21.

Lind, L.R., ed. *Lyric Poetry of the Italian Renaissance: An Anthology with Verse Translations*. New Haven: Yale UP, 1954. Contains a selection of fifteen poems, translations Ezra Pound, Hubert Creekmore, and

G.S.Fraser, including 1, 2, 13, 16, 18, 21, 22.

Nelson, Lowry Jr., ed. and trans. *The Poetry of Guido Cavalcanti*. New York: Garland, 1986.

Pound, Ezra, *The Translations of Ezra Pound*. London: Faber and Faber, 1953 (enlarged 1963).

Rossetti, Dante Gabriel, trans. *The Early Italian Poets together with Dante's Vita Nuova* (1861). Revised and republished as *Dante and his Circle* (1874). Now *The Early Italian Poets*. Ed. Sally Purcell, London: Anvil Press, 1981.

Wilhelm, James, *Medieval Song: An Anthology of Hymns and Lyrics*. New York: Dutton, 1971. Poetic versions of eight poems including 2, 18, 21, 22 and 23.

SELECTION OF RECENT CRITICAL MATERIAL

Critica del testo: Alle origini dell'Io lirico, Cavalcanti o dell'interiorità. IV / 1 (2001). Rome: Viella, 2001. Acts of the Conference held March 2001 ed. Guglielmo Gorni.

Guido Cavalcanti tra i suoi lettori, Proceedings of the International Symposium for the Seventh Centennial of his Death, Nov. 2002, ed. Maria Luisa Ardizzone. Fiesole: Edizioni Cadmo, 2003.

Ardizzone, Maria Luisa. *Guido Cavalcanti The Other Middle Ages*. Toronto: University of Toronto Press, 2002.

Beltrami, Pietro G. *La metrica italiana*. Bologna: Il mulino, 1991.

Boyde, Patrick *Dante's Style in his Lyric Poetry*. Cambridge: CUP, 1971.

Boyde, Patrick *Perception and passion in Dante's* Comedy. Cambridge: CUP, 1993.

Calenda, Corrado. *Per altezza d'ingegno: Saggio su Guido Cavalcanti*. Napoli: Liguori, 1976.

Calvino, Italo. *Lezioni americane: Sei proposte per il prossimo millennio*. Milan: Mondadori, 1993.

Cassata, Letterio. 'Per il testo delle Rime di Guido Cavalcanti (Contributi a una nuova edizione critica)'. *Italianistica* XIX (1990): 271-318.

Contini, Gianfranco. *Un'idea di Dante*. Turin: Einaudi, 1976.

Corti, Maria. 'Introduzione' in *Rime*. Guido Cavalcanti, ed. Marcello Ciccuto. Milan: Rizzoli, 1978.

Corti, Maria. *Scritti su Dante e Cavalcanti: La felicità mentale, Percorsi dell'invenzione e altri saggi*. Turin: Einaudi, 2003.

De Robertis, Domenico. *Il libro della Vita Nuova*. Florence: Sansoni, 1961.

De Robertis, Domenico. *Dal primo all'ultimo Dante*. Florence: Le Lettere, 2001.

Dragonetti, Roger. *Le technique poétique des trouvères dans la chanson courtoise. Contribution à l'étude de la rhétorique médiévale*. Bruges: De Tempel, 1960.

Favati, Guido. *Inchiesta sul Dolce Stil Novo*. Florence: Le Monnier, 1975.

Fenzi, Enrico. *La canzone d'amore di Guido Cavalcanti e i suoi antichi commenti*. Genova: il Melangolo, 1999.

Holmes, Olivia. *Assembling the Lyric Self: Authorship from Troubadour Song to Italian Poetry Book*. Minneapolis: University of Minneapolis Press, 2000.

Kleinhenz, Christopher. *The Early Italian Sonnet: The First Century*. Lecce: Milella, 1986.

Malato, Enrico. *Dante e Guido Cavalcanti: il dissidio per la Vita Nuova e il disdegno di Guido*. Rome: Salerno, 1997.

Marti, Mario. *Storia dello stil nuovo*. 2 vols. Lecce: Edizioni Milella, 1973.

Pazzaglia, Mario. *Manuale di metrica italiana*. Florence: Sansoni, 1990.

Pound, Ezra. 'Cavalcanti'. *Make it New*. London: Faber and Faber, 1934.

Rossi, Luciano. ed. *Rime*. Guido Guinizzelli. Turin: Einaudi, 2002.

Savona, Eugenio. *Repertorio tematico del Dolce stil nuovo*. Bari: Adriatica, 1973.

Savona, Eugenio. *Per un commento a "Donna me prega" di Guido Cavalcanti*. Rome: Edizioni dell'Ateneo, 1989.

Shaw, James Eustace. *Guido Cavalcanti's Theory of Love. The 'Canzone d'amore' and other related Problems*. Toronto: University of Toronto

Press, 1949.

Tanturli, Giuliano. 'La terza canzone di Cavalcanti: 'Poi che di doglia cor conven ch'i' porti'.' *Studi di filologia italiana*, xlii (1984): 5-26.

Tanturli, Giuliano. 'Guido Cavalcanti contro Dante.' *Studi in memorium Domenico De Robertis*. Eds Franco Gavazzeni and Guglielmo Gorni. Milan: Ricciardi, 1993. 3-13.

INDEX OF FIRST LINES